To Robert Sokan

These doctrines have developed forces which only await the day to break forth and fill the world with terror and astonishment. . . . Should the subduing talisman, the Cross, break, then will come roaring forth the wild madness of the old champions, the insane Berserker rage. . . .

—Heinrich Heine, 1834

Contents

Acknowledgments

I want to express my appreciation and thanks to the following people who, in various ways known or unknown to them, have helped me to complete this book:

My mother, Jessie Terrell, who gave me life, and who insured that I would know about the Lord Jesus Christ by taking me, as a young boy, to the Calvary Community Church in Maywood, Illinois (Evangelical and Reformed), and who sent me at significant cost and sacrifice to Illinois Wesleyan University; my brother, Bill Terrell, who has inspired me to think about many things through countless conversations about matters great and small, and who unfailingly encouraged me to keep working; my wife, Louise, who dragged me kicking and screaming into the world of computer technology and word processing, without which I would not have been able to work the manuscript into publishable form; Maggie Domalakes, whose careful reading of the manuscript helped me to correct many errors and stylistic irritants; and Robert Sokan, a great teacher at Illinois Wesleyan University who introduced me to two vital concepts—the direct object and the human condition.

Others who have aided me by their encouragement, challenge, reading, shared materials, phone calls, signatures, or prayers are: Kevin Terrell, Erin Terrell, Dr. D.R.

Ferrell, Dr. Glen Davidson, Dr. Erika Barton, Arch Lockee, June Nelson, Carol Surber, pastor Howard Keeley, pastor Lee Spitzer, Robert Lawrence, Dr. Liam Purdon, and Dr. Fred Brown. I am also grateful to the Board of Trustees of Doane College for two sabbatical leaves and to the helpful library staff at Doane.

My thanks to Princeton University Center of International Studies, Princeton, New Jersey, for permission to quote extensively from Beate Ruhm von Oppen's *Religion and Resistance to Nazism*, Research Monograph Number 35, Copyright 1971, Princeton University. Scripture quotations are from the Revised Standard Version.

Introduction

The Nazi eagle surmounts the encircled swastika, a dark silhouette against a gray sky. In the silent gloom it stands as a dread talisman over a savaged landscape. Then, with stunning power and suddenness, it shatters into myriads of pieces, exploding into nothingness. The symbol of Adolf Hitler's "thousand-year Reich" has become a thousand pieces of rubble, settling in every direction onto the apocalyptic devastation that is the city of Berlin. The Third Reich is dead.

The film that records the event described above is one of the most well-known documents of World War II. Its statement is clear, uncompromising, stern. Never again will this beast raise its power and, like a strutting Satan, move to-and-fro among the nations of the earth. But, half a century later, we find that the beast was not slain after all. The ideas and sensibilities that formed the cruel anatomy of national socialism remain and, indeed, seem to be rising from their graves to once again claim the allegiances of individuals, institutions, nations. How shall civilization, and specifically Christian civilization, confront this unsettling resurrection?

This question involves a look at history, specifically the evil epoch of the Third Reich and the Holocaust, arguably the central spiritual event of the twentieth century. What

ideas contributed to such an awful and mysterious outpouring of savagery by a modern nation? What are the
implications of those events, especially for the Christian
faith today? Why, over recent years, are we hearing increasing references to "fascism," and why is the Third
Reich regularly invoked as an example of warning to our
own society? What lies behind the talk of "ominous parallels"?

Fascism is a word that is much used in our day, even
overused. It is not a single idea, but rather a complex
synthesis. As one writer has stated, "The word, unfortu-
nately, has certain commode-like tendencies—the more you
stuff into it, the more it takes."[1] This book is not a study
of fascism as such, and the author is of the conviction that
the word is not really adequate to describe the unique
mystery of the evil that swept over Germany for a brief
period in the 1930s and 1940s of our century. Yet, here
it is appropriate to set some general characteristics in
mind that will be relevant to the discussion that follows. In
terms of sociopolitical realities, the concept of fascism
means the radical subordination of the individual to the
interests of the state, a system frequently called the "Corporate State." In the fascist arrangement, private industry
is allowed to exist, although only so long as enterprises
serve the agendas set forth by powerful forces of central
government. Understood solely in this limited sense, we
may readily perceive that certain aspects of our own national life are, to some extent, fascist. That does not mean,
however, that the United States is stoking up the gas ov-
ens! Indeed, a fascist nation like Italy, under Mussolini,
never got close to the peculiar evils of nazism. But, there
is more to fascism than economic arrangements, and these
elements are more central to the concerns of this book,
which focus on Christian life and thought in the shadow
of the Holocaust. Fascism is a spirituality, and, in the
following pages, I will seek to clarify how and why this
spirituality is diametrically opposed to a Christian worldview
and utterly incompatible with it. It will also be apparent,
as the discussion unfolds, that the premises underlying the

German ideology of the thirties are still with us and that the task of Christian faith in the present is well served by a consideration of its witness in its past confrontation with the utopian romance of antichrist.

No single individual symbolizes more powerfully, in popular imagination, the human tragedy of the Holocaust than the young Dutch girl, Anne Frank. But, when Anne Frank met her death at a young age in a Nazi extermination camp, she was not killed by some wild, disembodied insanity raised in defiance of modern intellectual and spiritual forces. Rather, the impulse toward "cleansing death" expressed in the gas that took her life, and millions of others, was largely the product of mainstream philosophical ideas informing Western consciousness in the aftermath of the European Enlightenment, through the eighteenth and nineteenth centuries. Although that epoch of our history is often praised for its ideals of tolerance, reason, and scientific progress, there is another side to the coin of modernity that was cast during the past two hundred years, comprising an intellectual and spiritual texture rooted in skepticism towards the traditional meaning structures of the West and the fanciful ideal of a man-wrought human perfectionism. It is my argument that this aspect of modern intellectual life released certain forces without which the Holocaust, generated by German national socialism, could not have been possible. In this sense, the Holocaust is a product of modernity's experimental search for meaning in the face of the vacuum left when mainstream intellectual life, following Nietzsche, declared the "death of God."

Ideas, sooner or later, have their consequences in the behavior of individuals and entire societies. What people believe in, and embrace as a worldview, is vital. The perspective of the author is that of a Christian layman who, while acknowledging the much trumpeted failure of Christendom during the years of the Third Reich, seeks to clarify how the very loss of belief itself, and the consequent erosion of faith in millions of Christian leaders and laity, left the door wide open in a nation of Christian

heritage to the demonic deceptions of a failed artist and
his National Socialist movement. And, although the perspective of this work is fundamentally cultural, dealing
with the realm of discernible ideas as they are manifested
in human life, I am ever mindful of the view of reality set
forth in the Christian Scriptures—that there is a mystery of
iniquity at work in the world, frightful and real, though
unseen, that works toward its goals of mayhem and destruction through deceit, incarnating in human culture
and institutions. As H.D. Leuner observed, in consideration of Hitler's persuasion of a whole nation to submit to
an unparalleled modern idolatry, it will all "make little
sense to many who do not believe in the existence of a
personal devil."[2]

Indeed, a consideration of the intellectual history and
the activities connected with the Third Reich will reveal a
pattern of principles that virtually define the character of
Satan as defined in the Bible, certainly a contributing
factor to the fact that even people who doubt the existence of a real, personal devil find the concept of the
"Satanic" relevant and meaningful. As Jeffrey Burton Russell
has reflected, the concept of radical evil traditionally expressed in the character of the devil cannot be outmoded
by any development of materialist philosophy or even scientific accomplishment, and, although actual belief in supernatural evil may have declined in modern times, the
modern world has certainly not noticed any decline in the
action of radical, Satanic evil.[3] The character of Satan
unfolds in the cultural milieu of the Third Reich. This
character is defined first and foremost by deceit, the clothing of death offered up as life, through the distortion or
denial of what God has spoken. It is the Prince of Darkness assuming the posture of an Angel of Light, the imaging ability whereby, in Hamlet's words, "the Devil hath
power to assume a pleasing form." There is the offering
of alternative altars, the worship of God's creation in denial
of the Creator himself, the exaltation of the creature who
would think to kill God and then stand in his place. Finally, there is the staggering, raging destruction of the one

creature who bears the Image of God, with special focus toward people whose spiritual roots associate them in particular with the revelation of the God who brings all things to the bar of judgement.

Whatever one may think about the supernatural, there is certainly something about the Third Reich that defies description and analysis that is tied merely to the canons of naturalism and materialism. After all that has been written about it, the Holocaust remains the gnawing puzzle of our century. Might it not be that so many attempts to comprehend it continue to draw blanks for the simple reason that we fail to put cultural and intellectual considerations in the deeper context of real, spiritual warfare? This book seeks to demonstrate the impact of ideas and the consequences that may, given specific conditions, flow from them, and in the process to clarify the relationship of intellectual life to spiritual discernment.

It is a central premise of this book that the Holocaust, and the Third Reich that brought it about, must admit an essentially spiritual understanding that has, at its core, the diminishing strength of allegiance to the biblical sources of knowledge concerning Jesus Christ. In taking this approach, I am seeking to address a charge, frequently stated in the secular milieu of our times, that the Holocaust is to be laid at the door of Christianity. Was not Germany a nation of profound Christian tradition, and had not that tradition absorbed centuries of anti-Semitic attitudes? Had not the Medieval Church fostered deeply set roots of Jew hatred? Martin Luther himself had written a nasty diatribe against the Jews. And, we have the spectacle of the enthusiastic support for Hitler in the German churches. In a further development, even the New Testament itself is held to express "anti-Semitic" attitudes.

The responsibility of Christendom for the Holocaust is an important and troubling theme. In recent years, we have seen a controversy over a Catholic convent's location at Auschwitz, an insensitive and blasphemous act in the eyes of some who see Christianity at the root of the Holocaust. In a similar vein, Jeffrey S. Sikar, reviewing Harry

James Cargas' *Reflections of a Post-Holocaust Christian*, refers to the Holocaust as "the appalling tragedy for which Christians were largely responsible."[4]

Indeed, it is almost a fashion in some circles to attribute virtually every evil in the world to Christianity, including the twentieth century's own version of hell on earth. It is also a fact that numerous Christian theologians and clergymen readily accept the notion of the guilt of Christendom. But, it is not my purpose to add to this posture. The position is well known, and it is embraced by many who were very directly involved and affected by those terrible events. I acknowledge the evidences that support such a position. Yet, we need to stop and consider that there is too little of positive remembrance of Christian integrity during the time period in view. Whereas I do not intend to whitewash or overlook the failure of Christian churches to exemplify the character of their Lord, neither do I feel called upon to emphasize them. I invite a different perspective. While recognizing that Christianity failed in many ways, we also need to give attention to the massive attack from intellectual quarters on the faith, and those who sought to embody it. Rather than merely asking questions about who failed or compromised, let us look as well to those who stood and why they did so. A minister I know once expressed his agony that, in regard to the Holocaust, we can find hardly any stories of Christian courage and integrity. He is wrong. I have been able to find many such instances, written about soon after the world war, and recent studies are uncovering more and more of them. Light is indeed being shed, finally, on great numbers of Christians who, along with many others, risked everything in courageous acts of mercy and help to the oppressed and despised. Stories of some of these people are included in these pages.

The confident pose of modern intellectuals is that "superstition," as exemplified in the doctrines of a supernaturally sanctioned church, has been discredited. Yet, we need to ask some questions of the so-called post-Christian mind. If, in fact, modern life has freed itself of the fetters of "superstition" and "dogma," a freedom that was being declared already in the nineteenth century, how is it that such a cataclysm as the Holocaust can be laid at the doorstep of an "irrelevant" faith? Don't we need to look elsewhere and confront the possibility that the Holocaust is a major cultural expression of modern life itself, with its premises grounded in foundational principles of "modernity"? Indeed, it is time that modern thought, with its heady claims of mature intelligence, faced up to the consequences of a wholesale rejection of the controls on human behavior implicit in Christian civilization. Fyodor Dostoyevsky warned, through his novel *The Brothers Karamazov,* that if God is dead all things are permissible. Is it mere coincidence, then, that in the full flush of humanity's disengagement from the God of the biblical revelation, the most unspeakable crimes are carried out? Is it mere coincidence that in the immediate wake of the rejection of God, the idolatry of the omnipotent state should arise? Is it mere coincidence that the premise of man's self-generated perfection should express itself in the massive "cleansing" of society of elements judged to be inimical to human progress and the realization of that perfection? And, is it mere coincidence that Christian churches offered a confused witness in a nation whose biblical scholars, building on anti-Christian philosophical premises, had launched the greatest frontal attack on historic Christian belief ever seen?

I don't think it is all mere coincidence and hope the following pages will explain why the Holocaust is firmly rooted in the intellectual premises so widespread and enthusiastically embraced by Western intellectual tradition through the nineteenth and twentieth centuries. The central essay, chapter 1, sets in place a basic historical overview of cultural and spiritual forces, while the remaining chapters are more sharply focused on the particular questions of anti-Semitism, the credibility of theistic belief in the wake of the Holocaust, the power of the artistic image to condition thought and action, and the degree to which our present cultural state continues to breed the possibilities of a repetition of such horrors. The book seeks to take seriously the exhortation to remember the relevant events while emphasizing the stream of ideas that fed them. This work is an introduction to a vast subject, with Christian faith as its primary doorway of concern. Hopefully, it will arouse curiosity in readers to look deeper and more fully contemplate the truth that ideas have consequences.

Endnotes

1. S.J. Woolf, ed., *European Fascism* (New York: Random House, 1968), 1.

2. Richard Gutteridge, *Open Thy Mouth for the Dumb* (Oxford: Basil Blackwell, 1976), 299.

3. Jeffrey Burton Russell, *The Prince of Darkness* (Ithaca, New York: Cornell University Press, 1988).

4. Jeffrey S. Sikar, review of *Reflections of a Post-Holocaust Christian*, by Harry James Cargas, *The Christian Century*, vol. 107, no. 11 (4 April 1990): 346-347.

∫ ONE ∫

Ideas and the Consequences

Scripture and history bear witness to the "mystery of iniquity." What is this mystery, and where does it originate? Moreover, how does it affect its influence upon human life in thought, culture, and institutional life? Ultimately, such questions are going to be answered from the position of one's fundamental assumptions about reality itself, whether those assumptions are held consciously or not.

And, no event of the twentieth century, or perhaps in all of history, challenges us to understand this mystery as does the Third Reich and the Holocaust it inspired. Not only do we ask how such a thing could happen, but we are puzzled as to why it should have happened in the particular nation of Germany, a nation that had been the center of the Protestant Reformation and that claimed as its national hero the great reformer himself. It had been a nation of significant achievement in the arts, philosophy, music, theology, and biblical studies and claimed a culture nourished by such voices as those of Martin Luther, Albrecht Dürer, Bach, Beethoven, Goethe, and Hegel. It was home to some of the world's most distinguished universities.

One conclusion is that cultural achievement is no guarantor of moral virtue or courage. The enduring interest in

the Third Reich is sustained by the manner in which the
whole event questions some of the cherished assumptions
of modern life, notably the notion that the salvation of
humanity will be accomplished through knowledge in the
arts and sciences. The Holocaust threatens all academic
and intellectual pride, defying "normal" academic questions and perspectives. The problem is so perplexing to
some that it is held to be some sort of "fluke," having no
explanation at all.

But, the Third Reich did not just happen. We need to
ask questions concerned with the nature of ideas and their
influence and what they contributed to the general climate
of thought during the nineteenth and early twentieth centuries that led, with a macabre logic, to the Nazi night-
mare.

Theologian Helmut Thielicke has observed that the
root issues are of a theological nature, an observation that
arouses attention to the disturbing truth that the German
churches, whom one would expect to have taken a stand,
not only proved ineffective in resisting the Nazi ideology
but gave it substantial support. Where was the spiritual
gift of discernment? By what deceptions were Christians
of the time left to grope sadly and heretically toward a
meaning system authored by powers of Darkness? How
could "enlightened" people of the twentieth century literally regard their Führer as a god with such exuberant neo-
paganism or as the historical expression of God as understood in some pseudo-Christian sense? What had happened
to the theological climate that would allow Germany's
churched population to depart so radically from the commands of Scripture—commands that clearly state the authority of Jesus Christ in all matters of Christian life, faith,
and conduct?

Moreover, what had happened to erode confidence in
Scripture itself and the Reformation doctrine of *sola
scriptura*? As for those who did offer resistance, upon what
principles did they stand as a basis for raising a voice?
These are questions that Christians must consider in any
reflection upon twentieth-century life. They are questions
that have a particular importance for Christianity, for

national socialism was much more than a mere political and economic, or even military movement. Nazism was a *religious* movement of the most sophisticated order.

Intellectuals and educators in the West are tempted by cultural chauvinism or naive views of human nature to see the Nazi epoch as an aberration, a movement running counter to all major trends in modern thought and intellectual life. Actually the reverse is closer to the truth. Such a thing as the Holocaust does not come about at random, as if in some intellectual vacuum. It is part of modern history and is surrounded with the whole milieu of ideas that constitute the modern world's search for new meaning structures in the face of the collapse of traditional theological belief. The full-scale assault on Christian theism, which began with the eighteenth-century philosophers of the Enlightenment and which strengthened through the nineteenth century, captured the imaginations of intellectuals and artists alike and laid the foundations of modern secularism. It is my thesis that, rather than constituting a movement running counter to the mainstream of modern philosophic and theological trends, national socialism represented a strange confluence of dominant post-Enlightenment attitudes regarding man, God, and religious truth and that it must be viewed as part of the de-sacralized modern world's search for alternative altars and surrogate faiths. Nazism and the Holocaust are best seen in the overall context of major intellectual assumptions and conclusions that characterized the growing and sophisticated skepticism of the nineteenth and early twentieth centuries. Although it may seem strange to say it, the Holocaust has a spirituality behind it.

Of foremost importance to this context was the gradual undermining of the credibility of Christian faith during the nineteenth and early twentieth centuries, first among the intellectual classes and educators, and then in the populace at large. The anti-supernaturalism of the Enlightenment had posited a bias against propositional revelation in Scripture. Not that all Enlightenment philosophers denied the existence of God; many recognized the reality of God but adopted a theology of Deism, in which God was held to have created the world with all the natural and moral laws "built in" to the system so that direct, divine intervention was not necessary. In such a system, the Christian claim that God had in fact spoken in specific ways through inspired prophets, apostles, and ultimately through the person of His incarnate Son, did not make sense. Although Deists retained much of traditional Christian morality, Deism set in place philosophic premises that fed a spirit of skepticism in regard to Christian claims of special and unique revelation. Related to the rise of Enlightenment rationalism, in which reason and science alone became arbiters of truth, the "higher criticism" of the Bible made the Scriptures appear to be faulty, historically incorrect, "mythological," and contradictory. Many of the conclusions of the higher criticism resulted not from real evidences of a scientific or textual character, but from the necessity of explaining biblical materials from the standpoint of a purely naturalistic philosophy that did not recognize either the ability or inclination of God to actually reveal Himself in tangible word or deed. Nevertheless, the conclusions of the higher criticism became the authoritative orthodoxy in biblical studies.

And, of course, there was the power of Darwinism. Evolutionary concepts were taken by many to furnish an explanation for origins that could reasonably exclude belief in the God of Creation proclaimed in the Bible. These primary forces were building an edifice of intellectual and spiritual life that, toward the end of the nineteenth century, supported a polemic against religion in general and Christianity in particular. The philosopher George Santayana captured the essence of this intellectual climate in his *Winds of Doctrine*:

> The present age is a critical one, and interesting to live in. The civilization characteristic of Christendom has not disappeared, yet another civilization has begun to take its place. We still understand the value of religious faith; we still appreciate the pompous arts of our forefathers; we are brought up on academic architecture, sculpture, painting, poetry, and music. We still love monarchy and aristocracy, together with that

picturesque and dutiful order which rested on local institutions, class privileges, and the authority of the family. We may even feel an organic need for all these things, cling to them tenaciously, and dream of rejuvenating them. On the other hand the shell of Christendom is broken. The unconquerable mind of the East, the pagan past, the industrial socialistic future confront it with their equal authority. Our whole life and mind is saturated with the slow upward filtration of a new spirit—that of an emancipated, atheistic, international democracy.[1]

Santayana is announcing a period of transition from a civilization grounded in biblical soil to what has come to be known as the "post-Christian" world. Implied is the idea that Christianity is in no way universal, but rather that it is just another system that has had its day. Notice also the abhorrence of tradition and a focus on the future as something that carries an authority superior to anything that has actually happened. Is it mere coincidence, we may ask, that a century dominated by the notion of human progress and visions of a future of perfected humanity in a perfected society should witness the most awesome crimes carried out in the name of utopia? Although it is certainly simplistic to "blame" the Holocaust on utopianism, we need not underestimate the power of this idea and vision to motivate human societies to force "perfection" along and energetically "cleanse" society of elements that cling too much to the consciousness of traditional ways.

A departure from traditional moral and spiritual authority was a cause for exhilaration among many of the turn-of-the-century intellectuals. Emerging was a new faith in the autonomy of man and an ongoing social progress. A new society could be envisioned which would derive its cultural expression, religious sensibilities, and moral fabric from the discoveries of science. Prominent intellectuals reflected in their writings a bold confidence in human scientific knowledge to provide a comprehensive framework for human life. Of note, as well, is the manner in which *society* was becoming the absolute goal of human effort and aspiration. The meaning of individual life was to be found only within the context of a distinctively modernist society, which rejected Christianity while joyously embracing an emergent secular spirit. As Michael Harrington has noted, the "risen god of sociology" was replacing the Judeo-Christian God, and this was "an event of enormous political importance."[2]

Such trends were visible in the intellectual and artistic life of various nations, Germany included. But, whereas France and other Western nations grounded their modernism in science and a classical humanism that retained many traditional values, Germany developed its vision of a new age more directly from a base in romanticist evolutionism that led to a radical departure from both historic humanism and Christianity alike. Two German intellectuals stand out in this respect. They are George W.F. Hegel (1770–1831) and Friedrich Nietzsche (1844–1900).

Hegel was Germany's most influential political thinker during the nineteenth century, and his philosophy has exerted an immense influence on modern thought in general. Not only political theory, but the disciplines of ethics, historiography, aesthetics, biblical studies, and theology have absorbed Hegelian assumptions. Central to Hegel's thought was his concept of history, which is expressed by the terms *dialectic* and *dialectical*. History is understood to be the unfolding process whereby one force or idea, identified as thesis, is confronted by an opposing force or idea, the antithesis. Out of the clash of thesis and antithesis arises a third force, that of synthesis, which itself becomes a new thesis.

As this concept came to be applied to theology, we see that Hegel's idea of God is an interesting distortion of the biblical picture. In Scripture, God transcends nature yet is actively involved in the affairs of mankind. He reveals His eternal nature and purpose in and through human events—action which itself constitutes history. But, God is a personal being distinct from the Creation and its activities. In Hegel, however, the transcendent nature of God is denied, and "God" is identified with history itself. Deity becomes wholly "immanent," or "in the world" and is indistinguishable from the historical process itself. History is the unfolding of the universal "Absolute Spirit," which is constantly in the process of realizing itself. History shows the evolution of Spirit, marching ever-onward to the fulfillment of its potential, with human institutions as the primary vehicle of this realization.

To the extent that this theological viewpoint impacted Christian thought, its influence was such as to militate strongly against historic Christian understandings of man, nature, God, and human institutions. The most radical difference, of course, is rooted in the matter of revelation. Christianity affirms a "once for all" revelation of the moral will and purpose of the God who transcends the world and judges it. In Hegel, and in subsequent theologies influenced by him, we see an understanding which virtually identified Deity with the world itself. Such a conception can retain no admission of biblical miracles, for there can be no manifestation of God apart from the natural course of events. This Hegelian immanentism was adopted by German biblical scholars and provided the framework for the conclusions of German "higher criticism" of the Bible. Under the "process" view of God, the centrality of the Bible for Christian faith declined; for if history itself constitutes the exhibition of Spirit working out its own potentialities, then no single historical event or person can finalize a divine revelation. Hence, the New Testament must be viewed, at best, as a tentative authority, a small part of the larger picture of thesis, antithesis, and synthesis.

If one accepted Hegel's view of God and history, the biblical record had to be explained and dealt with in terms other than those affirmed by Christian orthodoxy. To put it simply, if Hegel's concept were true, then the things that the Bible says happened could not have happened in any actual sense. Hence, began a process whereby Christian understandings were gradually detached from any base in literal fact. Building upon a Hegelian base, David Strauss, in his *Life of Jesus* (1835), denied all supernatural events in the life of Jesus and asserted that the story of Christ was an imaginative and mythological matrix of symbols embodying truths about human existence. Another Hegelian theologian, A.E. Biedermann (1819–85), drew a distinction between the "Christ principle" and the "Jesus of History," thereby segregating Jesus from Christ, while implying that there could be a "Christianity" substantially free of historical evidences and the biblical record. The word *Christ* became something defined merely as a symbolic concept related to man's evolving religious consciousness, rather than in accordance with the biblical presentation of Jesus. As we will see, these principles were to be used eagerly by proto-Nazi and Nazi ideologues in their desire to discredit the witness of the Judeo-Christian Scriptures.

Moreover, Hegel's notion that human institutions are the primary vehicle of the evolving Absolute Spirit exalted one institution above all others—the State. The State was, for Hegel, the very institutionalization of Divine Spirit in human life and was to be revered above all other institutions. Robert Waite has summarized the Hegelian concept of the State:

> In Hegel's special formulation—the Hegelian dialectic—the state is the higher synthesis which evolves from the clash of *thesis* and *antithesis*. The state synthesizes individual will and collective will, power and justice; it combines both moral right and physical force, freedom and authority. In fact, according to Hegel, freedom can fully exist only in a national state, and only in the state can moral purpose be fulfilled.[3]

Robert Nisbet calls Hegel "the preeminent philosophical influence in the glorification of human progress as attainment of national power" and the "transmutation of freedom from a state that has individual autonomy and rights as its essence to one in which the true measure becomes not autonomy or independence for the individual but his *willing* participation in a centralized absolute structure of power."[4]

Just as he had distorted the biblical presentation of God's activity in history, Hegel distorted the New Testament relationship of man to the State. In his epistle to the Romans, the apostle Paul had stated that governing authorities were instituted by God and that humanity was properly subject to these authorities. "For there is no authority except from God, and those that exist have been instituted by God. Therefore he who resists the authorities resists what God has appointed, and those who resist will incur judgement" (Rom. 13: 1–2).

However, the Scripture also places the state under the higher authority of God's law. It is to exercise power for good and execute wrath upon the wrongdoer, a commandment that presupposes an objective moral standard by which governments as well as individuals are to be judged. This is quite different from Hegel's deification of the State. In his various writings, Hegel referred to the State as "the divine will" and "the Divine Idea as it exists on Earth," the "march of God in the world." In this view, the individual person has no objective value or spiritual reality apart from the State. The State "is itself an individual, a mystic 'person' that swallows up the citizens and transcends them, an independent, self-sustaining organism, made of human beings, with a will and purpose of its own."[5] Although some historians object to the notion that Hegel is a proto-fascist thinker, the connection is well-drawn, because "for the Fascist, everything is in the State, and nothing human or spiritual exists, much less has value, outside the State."[6] Further, particular states represented at different times the will of the Absolute, and it was the Germanic nation that, for Hegel, represented the final stage in the development of nations in world history. Given this, his statements as written in the *Philosophy of Law* are particularly applicable to the exercise of German power toward other nations and ethnic communities:

> The Nation State is Spirit in its substantive rationality and immediate actuality; it is therefore the absolute power on earth. . . . The State is the Spirit of the People itself. The actual State is animated by this spirit in all its particular affairs, its Wars and its institutions. . . . The self-consciousness of one particular Nation is the vehicle for the . . . development of the collective spirit; . . . in it, the Spirit of the Time invests its Will. Against the Will no other national minds have rights: *that* nation dominates the World.[7]

This statement implies that culture plays the role of "messiah," for culture is the expression of the Absolute. The theme of national messianism is affirmed, in which it is implied that a particular national culture (for Hegel, the German culture), being the expression of the Absolute, claims a superiority over all others and possesses an intrinsic dispensation to rule.

Obedience to the State was, of course, familiar to German thought prior to Hegel, largely through Lutheranism. Hegel's deification of the State extended traditions of obedience to the secular authority, however, putting it on an idolatrous ground. To the extent that German theological thought mixed the Lutheran principles of obedience with Hegel's concept of the State as God, Christian understandings were seriously clouded, contributing to a confused and weakened moral witness during the reign of Adolf Hitler.

Hegel's philosophy became a base from which a modern redefinition of Christian faith grew. As modern theologians, pastors, and biblical scholars adopted Hegel as their working base, Christianity underwent subtle and destructive distortion. However, whereas the Hegelian thinkers sought to refashion theology in accommodation to Hegel, no such accommodation accompanied the thought of Nietzsche, whose writings breathe a virulent hatred for Christianity, leaving no room for synthesis.

Nietzsche was not primarily a political philosopher or a proponent of collectivist ideology. In this respect, his thought is the very antithesis of Hegel's. Nietzsche's thought is rigorously individualistic and primarily concerned with cultural regeneration rather than political or national power. In the words of Fritz Stern, he "tirelessly denounced German nationalism, anti-Semitism, and other proto-Nazi beliefs [and] never abandoned the individualistic premise of his thought." Stern notes that Nietzsche "loathed every collective tyranny."[8] Yet, it is certainly the case that Nietzsche's rhetoric provided easy fuel to the nineteenth century's anti-Christian sentiments and eventually to Nazi racial theories. Adolf Hitler is known to have visited the Nietzsche archives in Weimar on numerous occasions, and, as William Hubben observed, he "was made to serve the ideology of national-socialism, and an extensive popular literature grew quickly that added the philosopher to the long line of spiritual ancestors of the new political faith."[9] Writing of Nietzsche in the midst of World War II, Erich Kahler referred to him as "the man who started this revolution that threatens the foundations of the world of man."[10]

Nietzsche is most well-known for his declaration that "God is dead," a statement uttered by a madman in a parable that appears in his work *The Gay Science* (1882). The character in the parable expresses Nietzsche's view that the Christian God revealed in the Bible had become unworthy of belief and incredible for modern man. The death of the "old" God was, for Nietzsche, a reason for gratitude and great expectation. An admirer of the Enlightenment, which had established an anti-supernaturalist, rationalist, and skeptical point of view in religious matters, Nietzsche carried forth the Enlightenment's anti-Christian bias. His polemic against Christianity was accompanied by an equally intense criticism of existing institutions and systems. This is not difficult to understand, in that Christianity underlies the historic worldview and society of the Western world. For Nietzsche, the death of the Christian God meant the abandonment of the entire Western system of life itself, moral and institutional. This abandonment left man with no metaphysical obligations or certainties. There is a radical autonomy attributed to man in Nietzsche, which forthrightly rejects the biblical tradition that sees man as existing under the reality of an absolute moral law to which all are responsible. In Nietzsche, humanity becomes its own lawgiver and source of morality. No recognition is given to any transcendent power over man's moral conscience. He employed the concept of the "Superman" to express this autonomy, a being risen to superiority through the realization of values that reflect direct opposites of the traditional Christian virtues such as meekness, kindness, and sacrifice. The Superman comes with power, and the force of will, overcoming the "inferior" and "life-denying" values of the Christian faith. This is expressed in *The Antichrist*:

What is good? All that heightens in man the feeling of
power, the desire for power, power itself. What is
bad? All that comes from weakness. What is happi-
ness? The feeling that our strength grows, that an
obstacle is overcome. Not contentment, but more
power; not universal peace, but war; not virtue, but
forcefulness. The weak and ineffective must go under;
first principle of *our* love of humanity. And one should
even lend one's hand to this end. What is more harm-
ful than any vice? Pity for the condition of the ineffective and weak—Christianity. . . .

Christianity should not be beautified and embellished:
it has waged deadly war against this higher type of
man; it has placed all the basic instincts under the
ban; and out of these instincts it has distilled evil and
the Evil One: the strong man as the typically repre-
hensible man, the "reprobate." Christianity has sided
with all that is weak and base, with all failures; it has
made an ideal of whatever *contradicts* the instinct of
the strong life to preserve itself. . . . Christianity is
called the religion of *pity*. Pity stands opposed to the
tonic emotions which heighten our vitality: it has a
depressing effect.[11]

The complex, obscure, and often contradictory character of Nietzsche's writings raise barriers to any attempt
at systematizing his philosophy. Nevertheless, the impact
of three major ideas was overwhelming, these being the
death of God, the inherent potential of humanity to raise
itself to a higher state through spiritual and cultural
struggle, and the idea of the great man (the Superman).
As one observer has remarked, the attempt on the part of
Western civilization to act collectively on Nietzsche's premises was a major contributor to the modern crisis. Wilhelm
Grenzmann, writing for a postwar symposium on "Nietzsche
and National-Socialism" wrote:

The essential fact, which was to dominate the evolution of humanity for several decades, is that the Western world, through its ruling classes, attempted the
same experiment as Nietzsche. The general spiritual
trend, philosophical thought, literature and the plastic

arts, and political developments, all, in their various ways, reflect one and the same attitude to the world. . . . The forces which confronted Nietzsche were already set on the course which he opened up before them. Far from turning them back, he removed every obstacle from their path. So the stream became a torrent, and the torrent a raging waterfall.[12]

One of the more interesting aftermaths of Nietzsche's vision of the Superman was the manner in which this concept took root in German society. It is a classic example of how ideas make their way into the general consciousness of a society, from the mind of a single individual to a sustained presence in the thought of many. In this connection, Erich Kahler draws attention to the bizarre role and influence of the German poet, Stefan George, as a conduit of Nietzsche's worldview to the broader base of German society.[13]

George exemplifies the power of art and symbolism, to say nothing of personal charisma, in the transmission and influence of ideas. George was attracted to Nietzsche's thought, especially the notion of the Superman. Through George's influence, a generalized cult of "the great man" took root in German society, particularly among young people. For him, the great man was a totally integrated being, in the sense of the ideal of ancient Greece—a "complete, harmonious human being" in which mind and body are in perfect, complementary relationship. George desired to create a new elite, who would stand out in sharp contrast to common middle-class values and manners. Kahler notes that he patterned himself after great European heroes and poets, such as Alexander, Ceasar, Napoleon, Dante, Shakespeare and Goethe, and surrounded himself with a group of young men to give them a training that almost amounted to the breeding of a new type. One could often identify a disciple of George's by physical bearing and even facial resemblances to the poet. The devotees of Stefan George eventually came to occupy important chairs in the nation's outstanding universities. They also gained significant positions in public life. The movement begun by George actually came to constitute a

kind of secret state within the official political structure, a
"Secret Germany" with the principles of the cult as key to
the future.

Personally, Stefan George was a mysterious figure with
a compelling physical presence. Kahler describes him as
possessed of "a powerful, Dantesque head" with a slender,
graceful body. He wore simple but unusual apparel, similar to a clergyman's, and his manner "combined imperious
severity with the charm of a grand seigneur." It was his
practice to remain remote, aloof from the normal world of
activity, communicating with it only through his disciples.
Kahler sees a great significance in George's movement for
the future events that were to transpire in Germany:

> The impression that his movement made on the youth
> of Germany was of import for the future events, since
> George's followers offered an example of both ortho-
> dox devotion to a leader and manifest opposition to
> bourgeois society, and, above all, since they spread
> the idea of hero-worship, which was the kernel of
> George's teaching. The powerful creative man was
> considered the crown of creation; his deed as such
> was valued without regard for its effect. The fatal result
> was that this hero-worship became the link between
> Nitezsche's theory of the will-to-power and that base
> accomplishment of this will, the Nazi Reich. Trained
> to worship the hero as such, the youth of the country
> could no longer distinguish between true greatness
> and only brilliant criminality. . . . Nietzsche had intro-
> duced revolutionary anti-Christianism and the doctrine
> of a new elite. Stefan George tried to make this elite
> real, and thus he became an intermediary between
> Nietzsche's theory and the life of the people.[14]

Emerging out of this philosophical picture, grounded
in Hegel and Nietzsche, was the recognition of the proposition that man is the measure of all things. It is virtually
impossible to distinguish between God and man in these
philosophies. With Hegel, the activity of man *is* the activity
of God, whereas in Nietzsche the concept of God is thrown
out altogether, with humanity emergent, at least in poten-
tiality, as God.

However important the Hegelian deification of the State and Nietzsche's attack on Christianity, another important element contributed greatly to the formation of German religious attitudes that would leave the population intellectually and spiritually disarmed before the rise of nazism. The central premise here is the *subjectivity of truth*, and the central figure is the philosopher Friedrich Schleiermacher (1768–1834).

As in Hegel and Nietzsche, Schleiermacher's thought makes humanity the ultimate measure of spiritual truth. Because humans were thought to share a oneness with God through participation in the life of the spirit of the universe, inner sentiment was seen as a reliable guide to religious truth. Dogmatic matters, creeds, and the reliability of Scripture were peripheral elements for Schleiermacher, who is regarded by many as the "father" of modern liberal theology. Oddly, his principal concern was to defend Christianity in the face of the growing power of skepticism. He was concerned that the rationalist attacks upon Christian faith by the philosophers of the European Enlightenment would destroy Christianity. Rather than seek premises and evidences with which to defend the historic faith, Schleiermacher chose to refashion Christianity itself so as to make it appealing to the "cultured despisers" of religion. He had, then, an apologetic intent—that of preserving Christianity against the skepticism of the Enlightenment. His approach, however, was very strange. He replied to attacks upon Christian doctrinal understandings by saying, in essence, that doctrines and historical evidences were not important anyway, that what mattered was the inner spiritual consciousness of human beings, not the acts of God in history and the witness of Scripture.

Schleiermacher was the most influential force in German religion since Martin Luther. However, it is clear that he departed from Luther's recognition of the centrality of Scripture in matters of faith and belief. Schleiermacher's approach to Christianity established two important principles that were to have great impact. First, there was his disengagement of the content of faith from historical witness to events which could have a controlling or guiding result. This led to the second principle, the implicit notion that one could legitimately detach Christianity from its historic matrix of Scripture, creed, and doctrine and still have a valid claim to being a Christian. What Schleiermacher accomplished in reality was to promulgate a new religion altogether, while calling it "Christianity." This technique was of great convenience, eventually, to the Nazis, as we shall see, and has been an underlying problem of religious liberalism in the Christian churches throughout the twentieth century.

Although Hegel's theological distortions, Nietzsche's overt anti-Christianity, and Schleiermacher's emphasis on inner feeling and freedom from historic doctrine are central to an understanding of the theological and intellectual background to the Holocaust, other factors of equal importance contributed. These factors relate to specifically Germanic concepts of race, culture, and nationhood. What is the background of the virulent anti-Semitism evidenced in nazism, and how were theological concepts involved in the formation of this hatred? At this point, the subject becomes more deeply painful for all concerned with the broader history of Christian witness.

II

Jew hatred is one of the great mysteries of the world. In their book *Why the Jews?*, authors Dennis Prager and Joseph Telushkin call attention to the fact that at one time or another, almost every one of the world's great societies with a large Jewish population has regarded the Jews as enemies.[15] In that the Holocaust was carried out by a nation with a Christian history, this mystery has special meaning for Christians and calls for special attention. Whereas it is tempting for us to lay sole responsibility on the modern ethos of secularism and anti-Christian philosophy, we cannot avoid the ugly presence of anti-Jewish antagonism in Christian history.

This is not to give credibility, however, to the view of some (always anxious, it seems, to discredit the Christian faith) that Christianity was the root cause of the Holocaust or that the New Testament provided a groundwork for Nazi attitudes towards the Jews (see chapter 2). In actuality, Nazi ideologues and their predecessors were heavily dependent upon the traditions of Enlightenment rationalism, German romantic philosophy, and theological liberalism to underscore their fanatical hatred of the Jews. Nevertheless, it is true that the writings of Protestantism's founder, Martin Luther, were used quite directly by Third Reich propagandists. Nazi anti-Semitism was a strange mixture of these various elements.

According to Hannah Arendt, "antisemitism" is in fact a relatively modern, secular ideology rooted in the nineteenth century, and she distinguishes between older, religious Jew hatred and the modern, racialist dimensions of anti-Semitism. In the preface to her important work *Antisemitism*, she notes that the alien character of the Jewish people occurred in Jewish self-interpretation long before it became common in the later years of the Western Enlightenment and that Jewish scholars express outrage at evidences that reveal a Jewish tradition that is itself characterized by violent antagonism to Christians and Gentiles in general. She refers to the "nonfact" that Jewish separateness was exclusively the product of Gentile hostility. She suggests that the more accurate concept of history would recognize, between Jewish and Christian/Gentile civilization "a religiously predetermined, mutually hostile past."[16]

The Bible presents the Jews as a people of supernatural vocation. They are more than just another culture or world civilization. They exist for a purpose, by reason of the call of God. The ancient Hebrews were chosen by God to be a people set apart for the purposes of receiving God's special revelation concerning His redemptive purpose in human life. To the Jews were given covenant relationships and responsibilities toward God and man. Through the Hebrews came the revelation of the moral law of God and prophecies of a coming Redeemer. Biblically, the Jews are center stage in the history of God's redeeming activity. The bulk of the Christian Bible con-

cerns the origin and history of the Jews, and the vast
majority of the New Testament writings were penned by
Jews. The first Christians were Jews, and there is a pro-
nounced Jewish emphasis throughout the New Testament.
The gospel of John declares that "salvation is from the
Jews" (John 4:22), and Paul states that the Jews have been
entrusted with "the oracles of God" (Rom. 3:32). A lengthy
section of Paul's Roman epistle concerns the status and
destiny of the Jews. The Book of Revelation is heavily
Jewish in its imagery, reflecting many parallels to Old
Testament themes, especially those found in the Book of
Daniel. Of course, the culmination of God's revelation
comes in the Incarnation of Christ in Jewish flesh to shed
his blood for man's redemption from sin and judgment.

In view of this picture, it is difficult to erect a doctrine
of anti-Semitism on a biblical base. Jews are assigned a
priority in the matter of God's revelation, but they are not
marked off from other people in the matter of salvation.
Jews are not saved because they are Jews, nor are they
condemned because they are Jews. The biblical message is
clear, that all have sinned and thereby fall short of the
glory of God and are in need of the Savior (Rom. 3:23).
Further, in Christ there are no distinctions to be made
between Jew and Gentile (Gal. 3:28).

Anti-Semitism, or perhaps more accurately anti-Judaism, existed prior to Christianity. Long before the Medieval Church's expressed loathing of Jews, the ancient Greeks
and Romans had sown the seeds of historic Jew hatred.
This hatred was largely the result of the peculiarities of the
Jewish faith. Jews did not fit into the overall pattern of
society. They set themselves apart, refusing to worship the
pagan gods. Maintaining their own specific culture, they
practiced a separatism no doubt stimulated by memories
of the Babylonian captivity. This separatism, along with
the Jews' own disgust for the Gentile peoples, invited ridicule, scorn, hatred, and persecution. The refusal of Jews
to be assimilated into non-Judaistic religion and culture
seems to be the single unifying element running through
various manifestations of anti-Semitism, from the ancient

Greco-Roman paganism through the Medieval Church, to the Enlightenment philosophers and German racists.

Still, it is somewhat fashionable to ascribe modern anti-Semitism to Christianity, and there is no denying the force of this position. How do we account for the persistence and power of anti-Semitism in Western civilization given the central presence of the Christian church and its worldview undergirding our traditions? One could at least expect Christianity to have worked to alleviate existing hatred of Jews through its long centuries of cultural dominance. But, for the most part it did not happen.

Rhetoric against the Jews is found in early Christian history in the writings of some of the most important Church fathers. Through the centuries, the recurrent theme was that of the Jews as "Christ-killers" and "children of Satan." The crusaders of the eleventh and twelfth centuries regarded Jews as enemies as well as the Muslims they were sent off to fight, and, in encounters with Jewish populations, they would typically offer the alternative of conversion to Christianity or death. Massacres of Jews, anticipatory of the Nazi "final solution," were carried out even under the direct auspices of church leadership.[17]

But, was all this really "Christian" anti-Semitism? Is, indeed, such a thing even possible? Whereas it was certainly *church* sponsored, it may be more accurately ascribed to the peculiarities of the Medieval Church than to Christian faith itself. The Medieval period of our history is not known for its clarity of vision in respect to biblical authority, even though certain scriptural passages were utilized as a basis for anti-Jewish laws and persecutions. It is worth pointing out, as well, that *Christians* were also persecuted by the Church in Medieval times, as is seen in the histories of proto-Reformation movements and their leaders.

The Reformation era saw a return to the authority of Scripture, and a renewed emphasis on the Bible had the effect of increased toleration towards the Jews, although anti-Jewish sentiments certainly continued. Some Protestant countries, notably Holland and Britain, witnessed sig-

nificant improvement.[18] But, in Germany the writings of
Martin Luther were paramount, and although Luther initially condemned the Medieval Church's attitude towards
the Jews, his later writings echoed the abusive language of
the Christian past. Luther is, in fact, an important figure
in the history of anti-Semitism, although this is not widely
acknowledged or even known by many Christian laity today. Nevertheless, some writers of Holocaust literature go
so far as to call Luther a "spiritual ancestor" of the Nazis,
largely on the evidence that Hitler drew heavily on Luther's
pamphlet of 1543 titled *Against the Jews and Their Lies* to
justify his policies. Indeed, for Prager and Telushkin, Martin
Luther "constituted an important ally for the Nazis in the
carrying out of the 'Final Solution.'"[19]

Luther, however, was hardly a racialist in his approach
to the Jews. As Richard Gutteridge observes,

> It is absurd and unjust to present and to condemn
> Luther as a racial antisemite. He had no concern what-
> ever about the issue from the racial angle. It is equally
> ridiculous and unfair to insist upon making him di-
> rectly responsible for the misdeeds and atrocities of
> the Nazis. Luther. . . wrote brutally about the Jews,
> but there is no evidence that any Jew was executed at
> his behest or murdered with his approval. He is never
> to be found expressing his aversion to the Jews in
> biological terms.[20]

Luther's earlier writings about the Jews had struck a
positive tone in hope of winning many to Christ. He wrote
that the Jews "are the blood relatives, the cousins and
brothers of Our Lord," and that they "belong to Jesus
Christ much more than we do." In *Jesus Christ was Born a
Jew* (1523), Luther condemned the policies of the Medieval Church which had legislated the segregation of Jews
and Christians and had resulted in the destruction of Jewish property and lives.

> For our fools—the popes, the bishops, the sophists
> and the monks—these coarse donkey-heads, have hith-
> erto treated the Jews in such a way that any man who
> is a good Christian could well turn into a Jew. And if

> I were a Jew and saw such stupid rascals as these
> leading the Christian faith and giving instruction in it,
> I would sooner be turned into a swine than a Chris-
> tian. For they have treated the Jews as though they
> were curs with nothing in common with humanity.
> They continue to abuse them and take away their
> money even after they have baptized them as Chris-
> tians.[21]

Luther's apparent hope was that if the practices of the
Medieval Church were changed, Jews would accept Christ
as Lord and Messiah, but the frustration of this hope
brought an increasing bitterness toward the Jews. In 1543,
he penned one of the most infamous tracts in the history
of Christianity, *Against the Jews and Their Lies*, described by
one historian as a "hurricane of invective" and a "blazing
volcano of hatred and fury."[22] Luther complained that the
Jews were characterized by "lies, abusings, and curses,"
charges largely stimulated by Jewish references to the Vir-
gin Mary as a whore, Jesus as a sorcerer, and disparaging
views of the New Testament. He recommended in this
work such actions as the destruction of synagogues, schools,
homes, prayer books, and Talmudic writings, as well as the
expulsion of Jews from areas where Christians lived. Eventually, Adolf Hitler was to justify his policies toward Jews
through appeal to centuries-old policies of Christendom,
Catholic and Protestant alike. Surely, it is one of the greatest tragedies and ironies that Martin Luther, whose great
passion was the Word of God and salvation of human
souls, should have provided grist for the mill of one whom
he most certainly would have denounced as antichrist. We
also see the eagerness with which the Nazis drew upon
divergent sources in the formation of their ideology, utilizing simultaneously the thought of Nietzsche, who had
declared the "death of God" and the Christian worldview,
and Martin Luther, who had sought to recover biblical
understandings in the life of faith, a task that led directly
to the Reformation. As far as Luther is concerned in the
matter of anti-Semitism, it seems clear that he himself was
not always guided by the Scriptures whose authority he
had fought so valiantly to restore.

But, Nazi anti-Semitism was furnished by other sources
as well. By the time of the Nazi ascent to power, Europe
in general had developed a strong brand of secular anti-
Semitism, rooted in the French Enlightenment and nine-
teenth-century evolutionism.

The nature of Enlightenment anti-Semitism has been
clarified by Arthur Hertzberg in his book *The French Enlightenment and the Jews*. According to Hertzberg, modern
anti-Semitism developed within the Enlightenment tradition and was often linked to the more generalized attack
of the rationalist philosophers upon the Bible. The Jews
were "desupernaturalized," no longer to be understood as
a people who had been historical vehicles of God's revelation. This accorded with the Enlightenment assessment of
Scripture as an incoherent mixture of inaccurate history,
myth, and primitive superstition. To Voltaire, the
Enlightenment's leading voice, the Jews "surpassed all
nations in impertinent fables" for which they deserved to
be punished. Hertzberg notes that Voltaire abandoned
entirely the older religious attack on the Jews as "Christ-
killers" and moved to a new principle upon which to base
Jew hatred, namely their inherent character. Voltaire and
other philosophers scorned the Jews and Christians alike,
on the same basis, holding that neither could be readily
assimilated in a new society grounded in the cultural values and philosophic outlook of classical antiquity. Although
some distinction was made between "modern" Jews and
"ancient" Jews, it was apparent to the Enlightenment intellectuals that contemporary Jews were committed to their
historic traditions, grounded as they were in supernatural
religion and revelation. Leading the Enlightenment's anti-
Jew mentality was Voltaire, who "was consistently understood on all sides to be the enemy of the Jews of the
present as well as those of the past. His writings were the
great arsenal of anti-Jewish arguments for those enemies
of the Jews who wanted to sound contemporary."

Hertzberg writes that

> an analysis of everything that Voltaire wrote about
> Jews throughout his life established the proposition

that he is the major link in Western intellectual history between the anti-semitism of classical paganism
and the modern age. In his favorite pose of Cicero
reborn he ruled the Jew to be outside society and to
be hopelessly alien even to the future age of enlightened men.[23]

Moreover, the Enlightenment's emphasis on the need
to remake man to fit into a new modern society, contributed to modern totalitarianism and laid the groundwork
for secularized persecution of the Jews.

The idea of remaking men to fit properly into the new
society was the seed-bed of totalitarianism. The notion
that the new society was to be a reevocation of classical antiquity was the prime source of post-Christian
anti-semitism in the nineteenth century. The vital link,
the man who skipped over the Christian centuries and
provided a new, international, secular anti-Jewish rhetoric in the name of European culture rather than religion, was Voltaire.[24]

But, the decades preceding the rise of national socialism were alive with evolutionism as well, presenting a vision of human progress linked to racial conceptions that
obliterated the traditional Christian conception of the unity
of all human races as expressed in Scripture (Acts 17:26).
Central to this notion of human progress through racial
struggle was the thought of the Frenchman Joseph
Gobineau who, in his *Essay on the Inequality of the Human
Races* (1853–55), posited the issue of race as the primary
moving force in human history. Then, of course, there was
Charles Darwin in England, whose *Origin of Species* (1859)
revolutionized the biological sciences. Robert Proctor cites
Darwin's theory as "a watershed in the history of biological determinism in general and scientific racism in particular," for prior to Darwin "it was difficult to argue against
the Judeo-Christian conception of the unity of man."[25] As
Darwinian ideas came to dominate the later nineteenth
century, the notion of universal struggle came to apply to
the destiny of civilizations in the thinking of the so-called
Social Darwinists. Ernst Haeckel, a biologist and philoso-

pher much enamored with Darwin, popularized these ideas in Germany around the turn of the century through writings that had immense currency. Hitler read with interest Haeckel's *Die Weltrathsel* (1900), in which he had declared the validity of Darwin's concept of life evolving through "the struggle for existence." He wrote that now, in modern times, "nobody today speaks any longer of a 'moral order,' or of a personal God, whose 'hand hath disposed all things in wisdom and understanding.' The same applies to the whole field of biology, to all organic nature." Haeckel made the important denial that, as applied to man, the Darwinian notion of the survival-of-the-fittest meant "survival of the best" in a moral sense. So, "the entire history of the organic world goes to prove that side by side with great progress toward perfection, we find, at all times, instances of decline toward lower stages." He makes reference to "branches of the human family which, as nations and races, have struggled for survival and progress."[26]

The implication here would seem clear. Not all human beings represent races *worthy of life*. Some are "low" or "retrograde," whereas others represent human progress, material and moral. The struggle for racial survival and supremacy is joined, with human destiny as the ultimate issue.

Hence, from the mainstream of Western spiritual and intellectual life a great catastrophe was being hatched. The lie of Eden that "ye shall be as gods" was finding new body in philosophies of history, culture, and race. How did these trends come together, forming that peculiarly virulent ideology that was to poison twentieth century experience in Nazi Germany? This question leads to a consideration of specifically Germanic elements growing out of German romantic thought, and an emerging "German religion" which was coming onto the stage of history—the cult of the Völk.

III

The intellectual developments we have noted cast the Western world into an increasing spiritual crisis. The older meaning structures of the Christian faith were eroding under the attacks of the apostles of Absolute Reason, the belief that science constituted the sole path to truth, and the emergence of distorted, arbitrary theological inventions. For the professional intellectuals and thinkers in the universities as well as the proverbial "common man," a new context within which the meaning of life could be affirmed was being sought.

In Germany, this context came to be dominated by concepts of race, blood, and soil, and a peculiar form of messianism grounded in Teutonic myth and folklore. An early statement of this consciousness was made by the philosopher Johann Fichte (1782–1814), who was roughly contemporary with Hegel. In his *Addresses to the German Nation* (1807–08), he wrote:

> To have character and to be German undoubtedly mean the same. . . . All comparisons between the German and the non-German are null and void. . . . We are the chosen people. Chosen by God . . . with a moral right to fulfill our destiny by every means of cunning and force.[27]

Fichte's philosophy makes no distinction between the individual, the nation, and the State. The individual's moral nature is nurtured in relationship to the community, and the State gives protection and identity to both individual and society. The State, then, is of absolute significance and, as Robert Nisbet observes, it is held to be an expression of cosmic evolution itself, "as much an inexorable outcome of a long evolutionary process as anything to be found in the world of nature."[28]

There is in Fichte's words a theme of "blood superiority." This idea was taken up by later Nazi thinkers and was embraced as well by German theologians. The theme, however, was given two different emphases, the biological and the cultural. Some German philosophers emphasized simply the superiority of Germanic achievement in art and intellectual life, while others came to include the concept of racial destiny. Fichte also hinted at the theme of German messianism in which the German people are thought to possess a divine mission to mankind in general.

What was to take possession of the German consciousness was a militant romanticism. Romanticism, as a mode of consciousness, is grounded in an exaltation of mystery, inner feeling, and a sense of limitless expansion—a "yearning for the infinite." Precise definition is contrary to the romantic spirit. Although romanticism takes various forms in European culture, the center of a romantic mode of existence is a defiance of limitation. In Germany, this expansive consciousness came to stress the individual's significance as part of a larger "organism" such as the race or nation, through which destiny is mediated. Theologically, the romantic consciousness repudiated doctrinal understandings, a development which was to have devastating consequences for the German church and nation. Hence, we note Peter Viereck's cogent observation that "we can enter the ideological house that Hitler built only by entering through the underground passage—apparently far off, apparently un-Nazi—of romanticism."[29]

According to this way of thinking, the Divine Spirit is manifested in the spirit of a people, in their collective genius and total culture or *Völksgeist*. Out of this concept was born a virtual religion of the *Völk*. This religious attachment to the *Völk* deified the race and nation so as to turn the state into a spiritual and religious entity all its own. In the nineteenth century, the biblical theme of Fall and Redemption was construed to suggest a pattern of decay and regeneration among nations. To the German romantic thinkers, European civilization was in decay, as witnessed by what they regarded as the abstract rationalism of the French Enlightenment. In the face of the West's intellectual convulsions, Germany developed a kind of communal mysticism which contained its own Teutonic concept of a "chosen people," called to redeem civilization from its decadence. Accompanying this idea was an attack upon non-Germanic elements of civilization which were central contributors to Western decadence, namely Jewish elements and traditions of Latin Christianity. Luther's Reformation was interpreted as a call for Germans to regenerate Christianity itself, a regeneration that was dependent upon the realization of Germany's unique destiny. According to such thinkers as Fichte, a German-stimulated era reflecting the very order of the cosmos was about to break upon the stage of history. With Fichte and Hegel as intellectual pillars, the concept of a German religion mixing Christianity with Teutonic destiny and German nationalism increased in power through the nineteenth century.

Such a belief in a Germanic faith was built upon the underlying vision of Völkish thought, which was considerably more complex than a mere concern for national destiny or even religious regeneration. Neither German nationalism nor the desire for a specifically German religion led necessarily to the Holocaust. Rather, the key ingredient is the relationship between the romantic religious mood and anti-Semitism. While Voltaire had secularized anti-Semitism and based Jew hatred on the assumption that they could not be assimilated into the society of an emerging new age, Völkish tradition revealed a similar attitude in perceiving the Jew as utterly at odds with the soul of German life. According to the Völkish ideology, man's relationship to nature, to the land, was of paramount importance, for nature itself was understood to manifest the cosmic Life Spirit.[30] Man possessed spiritual rootedness to the extent that he had contact with the land and its historical associations. Such rootedness was seen as necessary for a properly functioning human soul, and to be without it was to be deprived of the cosmic life force. In this regard, urbanization and industrialization comprised a threat to the very soul of Germany. As for the Jews, they were associated with the latter realities. They lived in the city, detached from any real rootedness and, therefore, any real spirituality. To the extent that Jews fostered urbanization, they were encouraging people to detach themselves from their spiritual source, the land. The Jew himself was seen as a wanderer and, therefore, a soulless creature lacking real humanity. His influence upon German life could only hinder the progress of Absolute Spirit toward its realization and the fulfillment of German spiritual destiny.

The Völkish vision is, of course, a long way from Christian thought, and its "cosmic spirit," struggling to realize itself, can by no stretch of the imagination be identified with the biblical God. Yet, the kind of thinking evidenced in the Völkish mythology came to be seen as a "Christianity," based on simple feeling and the exaltation of the peasant. It was "a Christianity not hemmed in by theological orthodoxy and thus free to fuse with the life spirit originating in the pantheistic cosmos."[31] Freed of doctrinal considerations tied to actual Christian history (a vision fostered by Schleiermacher), the new Germanic faith began to emerge, yet under the name of "Christianity." Clearly, the liberalizing thought of Hegel and Schleiermacher, both of them Lutherans, served this confusion. Increasingly, "Christianity" was emptied of historic doctrinal content, to be refashioned according to Germanic thinking, which constituted, in essence, a rival faith. This trend becomes clear in the thinking of two individuals who, although they are not major figures in the history of thought, exerted a powerful influence on the development of the German ideology. They are Paul de Lagarde (1827–91) and Julius Langbehn (1851–1907). With these two men, Völkish concepts became more systematized.

Fritz Stern, in *The Politics of Cultural Despair*, sets the work of these men in the context of a radical criticism of modern culture. Modernity, or what was then referred to as "liberalism," was characterized by debilitating urbanization and middle-class mediocrity. Its emphasis on individualism worked to break down communal bonds, and capitalism (which they associated with Jewish influence) was establishing a soulless materialism.

> Their one desire was for a new faith, a new community of believers, a world with fixed standards and no doubts, a new religion that would bind all Germans together . . . [and] a *Führer* who would embody and compel unity and expunge all domestic conflicts. Their final vision was a new German destiny, a Germany which, purged and disciplined at home, would stand forth as the greatest power of the world.[32]

Lagarde's hopes for a Germanic religious faith were accompanied not only by a rejection of the Jews, but traditional Christianity as well, Catholic or Protestant. Catholicism was dangerous for Lagarde because it was international, breaking down national distinctions. As for Protestantism, Lagarde repudiated the Reformation principle of an authoritative Bible. For him, the significance of Luther's thought was that the great reformer had stressed the need for a national religion in Germany. The Bible itself, though, which had been so central to Luther's reform, had to be discredited. In this task, Lagarde drew from the conclusions of the German "higher criticism" and radical theologians, most notably Ludwig Feuerbach, D.F. Strauss, and Ernst Renan.[33] These scholars had engaged in the so-called quest for the historical Jesus, in which they assumed a purely naturalistic origin for the Christian faith, beginning with a normal human being named Jesus, whose life and career had later been overlaid with supernaturalism and myth. Following the higher critics, Lagarde asserted that Christianity had developed its doctrinal positions without respect to the actual teachings of Jesus. The primary culprit of this distortion was St. Paul, who covered over the message of Jesus with Jewish ideas. Christ, claimed Lagarde, had simply stressed a religion of "inner spirituality" and "personal revelation."

Evangelical scholars have argued for many years that the "higher criticism" was nothing less than a frontal attack on the Christian faith itself. There can be little question that it served well those who, like Lagarde, sought to undermine the biblical basis of religious faith. The presuppositions underlying this movement were drawn from Hegelian concepts of historical development combined with an anti-supernaturalist bias, and they generally forced scholars to conclude that major events of the Bible could not have actually happened and that traditional assignments of authorship were not accurate. As their conclusions were popularized by Julius Wellhausen in the later nineteenth century, they became the basis of an "orthodoxy of skepticism" regarding the historic truth claims of

Christianity. But, according to Arthur A. Cohen, the higher criticism of the Old Testament can also be understood as a "higher anti-Semitism," seeking to disengage Christianity from its authentic Jewish roots. According to Cohen, the nineteenth century revolution in biblical studies begun by the German school of higher criticism represented an "onslaught" on the Hebrew Bible that was guided by an ideological impulse to demean the Judaic element in Christianity.

> In response, it would seem, to the position of the Enlightenment, it became the concern of Protestant Biblical scholarship to disentangle Christianity from its Jewish roots, to split off the Christian experience from that of Judaism and at the same time to naturalize the humanity of Jesus. It became commonplace in this movement of thought to demonstrate that what appeared to the lights of Reformation theology to be most generous, humane, charitable in classic Judaism was really a contribution from outside, whereas indigenous Biblical Judaism was violent, self-righteous, obsessionally paranoid.[34]

Utilizing the liberal scholarship of the nineteenth century, Lagarde established a base for separating the "Christ of faith" from the "historical Jesus" and the biblical witness. Having done so, he was free to put whatever content he found convenient into the "Christ" concept. In this, he followed the patterns of Protestant theological liberalism. For Lagarde, Christ was merely a symbol for a person infused with the dynamic life spirit. Lagarde went on to draw parallels between Christ's association with the community of disciples and the concept of the *Völk*. The life force becomes real and significant only through a community—and Germany was that community. This maneuver manifests a fundamental tendency in Völkish thought, relative to Christianity, which witnesses the substitution of the image of the *Völk* for the person and function of Christ.[35] The Life Force ("God"), which had been manifested in Christ, had continued to reveal itself through history and now was present in the *Völk* through whom the kingdom of God was to be found. This primacy of the *Völk* is combined in Lagarde with the typical Völkish hatred of the Jew, which during Lagarde's lifetime was increasingly intense through years that saw the growth of Germany into a national political entity. For Lagarde, Jesus' words "I am the Son of Man" really meant "I am not a Jew,"[36] and his references to Jews as "trichinae" and "bacilli" calling for extermination became prophetic.[37]

Langbehn continued the separation of religious affirmation from historical sources. Lagarde had sought the groundwork for his ideas in the work of biblical scholars, whose conclusions he thought were valid. At the very least, they were convenient. But, Langbehn's writings were more immediately mystical, drawing upon the pseudo-Christian theology of the Swedish genius Emmanuel Swedenborg and the occult Theosophy of Madame Helena Blavatsky. Although Langbehn rejected much from these philosophies, he drew upon them to elaborate the Völkish ideology, which stressed the mystical relationship between humanity and the cosmos. Langbehn limited this relationship to the people of the region of northern Germany, however, whereas Swedenborg had located it in Christ. As with Lagarde, Langbehn substituted the *Völk* for Christ, and, like Lagarde, he longed for a great leader that would personally embody and express the longings implicit in the *Völk*.

Langbehn's major, and most popular work, was a strange book entitled *Rembrandt als Erzieher* (Rembrandt as Educator), which is described by Fritz Stern as a "wearisome diatribe" possessing a "heightened sense of chaos" reminiscent of the later works of Friedrich Nietzsche.[38] In it, Langbehn expressed the view that art was the key to spiritual regeneration of the *Völk*, with Rembrandt as a symbol of the "hero artist." The book did not have much at all to do with the actual Dutch painter of the seventeenth century, but Langbehn saw in Rembrandt's art the expression of mystical emotion that was fundamentally at odds with debilitating aspects of modern culture—technology, commerce, materialism. "Rembrandt's chiaroscuro

suggested the mysterious depths and contradictions of
human life, and for Langbehn this was clear proof that the
knowledge intuited by art was far superior to the knowledge deduced or researched by science."[39] He envisioned,
then, a new age in which art would determine politics,
with a spiritually elevating art springing from the life of
the *Völk*. However, central to this regeneration and rebirth
was the Führer, who in his own person would embody the
spiritual aspiration of the people and provide the focus of
cultural unity. The new society would have no room for
certain people, notably Jews, whom Langbehn characterized as having "no character, no home" and as "a piece of
humanity become sour."[40] As regards to Christianity,
Langbehn embraced the contemporary tendency to view
all religion as constantly in process of evolution, with no
fixed or absolute premises.

In *The Crisis of German Ideology*, George L. Mosse views
the significance of Lagarde and Langbehn for the development of German religious consciousness:

> In their respective works Langbehn and Lagarde pro-
> vided a systematic framework for future Völkish
> ideas. . . . They accepted the romantic impetus and its
> premise: the primacy of man's inner emotions, which
> were the genuine indicators of his personality. As a
> corollary they stated that this inner spiritual nature of
> man, properly circumscribed by the *Völk* could trans-
> form the evil world of contemporary reality. . . . Reli-
> gion—specifically a German religion—was the expres-
> sion of a romantic longing. . . . That the two fathers of
> the Germanic religion rejected the dogmatic bases of
> orthodox faiths and identified with a dynamic spiri-
> tual force that worked within the individual and the
> *Völk* only reflected a general condition of religious life
> in an industrializing German state. Their approach to
> the predominant Protestant faith prefigured a change
> that eventually came about toward the end of the
> century.[41]

The Germanic religion, then, was not Christianity at
all, even though it may have retained certain key words

and phrases related to Christian faith—words like *Christ* or *salvation*. It was a combination of several nondoctrinal religious themes detached from Christian historical moorings. The way had been substantially prepared through the undermining of the historic faith by the higher criticism, which insisted upon fitting the biblical literature into a worldview grounded in naturalism and Hegelian evolutionism. Mosse observes that "Christianity, already weakened by a prolonged attack by the school of Biblical higher criticism, stripped of dogma and historicity, was sucked into the all-pervasive Germanic faith."[42] In a similar vein, Arthur Cohen notes that the higher criticism, to the extent that it separated Christianity from its Old Testament roots, "de-Judaized" Christian theology, the consequences of which could not be more evident than in "the pitiful inability of the Protestant churches to oppose German National Socialism." Citing the liberal scholarly tradition, Cohen writes that "the purge of Christianity of its Jewish elements was disastrous. If that was Judeo-Christian tradition—in the spirit of Wellhausen, Kittel, (and even most recently Bultmann's *Primitive Christianity*)—the world could not abide it again."[43]

By the time that Adolf Hitler emerged in Germany, the theology of the nation had been thoroughly perverted, and its basis for confidence eroded, a situation that worked easily to blur the distinction between an authentic Christian faith and the Völkish tradition. Hence, Hitler could come to power proclaiming that he and the Nazi party stood for "positive Christianity." Hitler, like all too many of Germany's theologians, felt free to redefine Christianity to suit his own purposes and philosophy, utilizing freely the words familiar to Christianity and thereby playing upon its authority, while pouring private and nonhistorical meanings into them. When Hitler spoke of "Christianity" he meant, in reality, the Germanic Völkish faith, and many theologians and churchmen agreed. The foundations for such distortion had been laid in the seminaries—fertile environment for the higher criticism and the "liberal" theology.

It remained for a non-German, however, to bring to a climax the distortion of Christianity into a religion of Aryan supremacy, the Englishman Houston Stewart Chamberlain (1855–1927). His ideas came to a mature expression in a monumental work entitled *The Foundations of the Nineteenth Century.*

Chamberlain, although an Englishman by birth, was attracted to Germanic culture and eventually became a citizen of Germany. His contribution to nazism was two-fold. First, he worked out a purely racial conception of history, in which the Germans were seen as superior and specially gifted. Secondly, building upon the theoretical foundations of higher criticism and theological liberalism, he separated the concept of "Christ" from its biblical and historical foundations and in the process transformed "Christ" into a Teutonic hero.

According to Chamberlain, a three-fold heritage was left to the world by the ancients. There was Greek art and philosophy, a tradition joined by the accomplishments of Roman law. Third, there was the personality of Christ. There were also three races, two of which were pure. The pure races were the Jews and the Germans, while the third represented a racial confusion of half-breed Mediterranean peoples whom Chamberlain called the *Völkerchaos.*[44] The ancient heritage had been handed down in a distorted form through the Jews and the Mediterranean chaos of peoples, whose blood was mixed. Chamberlain understood the German race to be struggling to receive the true ancient heritage, wresting it from its usurpers and corruptors. The Jews were congenitally incapable of understanding Christ, and the Mediterraneans distorted everything. The German struggle triumphed in the Reformation era, when the Germans opposed the Roman church and began to affirm the concept of a German Christianity. From the year 1200, a new race of people, the Teutons, was coming into being, and it was this race that was the true heir to the ancient heritage and which would build a new civilization to overcome the distorted conceptions of the other races. The principal antagonists of the Teutons, however, were the Jews, inasmuch as they were the only other race that had retained its purity. In *The Foundations,* Chamberlain presented the Jews as an alien people contriving to dilute the racial purity of the Teutons through intermarriage of Jewish women with European men, while sustaining their own racial purity by forbidding intermarriages of Jewish men with European women.[43] Therefore, the German was in a life and death struggle with the Jew. Further, the Jews were deficient in religious instinct. Chamberlain saw the Old Testament commandments, rituals, and ordinances as superstitious formulas which gave evidence of the Jews' lack of true spiritual inwardness and emotion.

The most unique feature of Chamberlain's philosophy was in regard to Christ and Christianity. His avowed task was to separate the figure of Christ from all historical Christianity. In this, his thinking resembles the liberal theological tradition of freely rejecting doctrinal contexts of understanding.

> [He] drew up a project for a religious community of the liberal protestant type, with a "cult" where the formal and impressionable elements, centered round the person of Christ, were more important than the intellectual, rational, and ethical elements. In brief, this would be a religion with hazy outlines that contrived by avoiding the hardening effects of logic, to interpret the unknown through the medium of man's senses, heart, and imagination.[46]

For Chamberlain, doctrine was "rationalistic" and artificial. "Christ," for Chamberlain, came to symbolize and embody the emerging glories of the German race, and *The Foundations* became a leading source of authority for the Völkish movement towards a Germanic spirituality. The importance of Chamberlain's work was recognized by Hitler himself, who visited him in 1927 as the Englishman lay sick and dying. Hitler also attended Chamberlain's funeral.

Chamberlain's new "Christ" was not, of course, a Jew. He denied Christ's Jewishness on the grounds of Jesus' Galilean background which, he argued, indicated a racial mix in Jesus. Therefore, Christ could not have been in a strict sense a Jew. Moreover, the religious nature of Christ was contrary to Judaism. Christ embodied the Aryan spirit which was "joyous" and "full of animal spirits," with an instinct "to seek the core of nature in the heart." Chamberlain went so far as to say that Christ most probably did not possess one drop of Jewish blood. Consequently, although of no certain race, Christ was related to the Aryans by his attitude and religious thinking and became "the God of the young, vigorous Indo-Europeans" who represented the dawn of a new culture, "a culture at which we have still to toil long and laboriously until some day in the distant future it may deserve the appellation 'Christ-like.'"[47]

It was Alfred Rosenberg who finally drew together the premises of Völkish thought and opened an all-out assault on historic Christianity in his book *The Myth of the Twentieth Century*. Reiterating familiar themes, Rosenberg attributed to the apostle Paul an unhealthy "Judaizing" tendency in early Christianity that distorted and diverted primitive Christianity from its true source and meaning. The true Christ was the Aryan hero of H.S. Chamberlain. This "Christ" figure was a "Christ of faith" separated from all scriptural and historical context, a figure who embodied "warrior virtues." According to Rosenberg, true Christianity would lead men to heroic superhumanity. If necessary, force and violence must be utilized. This "true" Christ had been distorted by Paul into a weak figure who functioned as mediator between God and man and who called men to be saved from their sin and who set forth commands to humility and brotherhood.[48] The concept of sin, naturally, could have no place in such a scheme. For Rosenberg, the sense of sin was a sign of racial bastardization,[49] and, inasmuch as Catholicism and Protestantism both maintained the doctrine of human sin in the face of a righteous God, they had to be opposed and destroyed. Taking their place would be the Völkish, "Germanic" spirituality, which Hitler proclaimed under the banner of "positive Christianity."

It was easier for Rosenberg to justify an attack on the Catholic church than upon Protestantism. Catholicism, being international in scope, was by nature antithetic to "Germanism." The Lutheran churches, however, constituted a different problem. Even though Christian theology had undergone a grotesque distortion under the influence of Hegel, Schleiermacher, Strauss, and the Völkish thinkers, the fact remained that Martin Luther was still the great national hero of Germany. He had opposed Rome and the papacy, and his reformation had signalled the beginnings of a Germanic national consciousness. It was this latter theme that Rosenberg stressed. True Lutheranism was Germanism! Germany had made the mistake of accepting "Pauline" Christianity and had committed the offense of maintaining contact with Judaism through its stress on the Bible. The true origins of Lutheranism lay in a national, completely Germanic religion that would negate all concepts of sin and erect instead an aggressive heroism expressive of Völkish spirituality. Such theories led eventually to the formation of the German Christian movement, first organized in 1932, which set out to define what "believing in Christ" would really mean for a German and to separate "Christianity" from all contact with Judaism and the Old Testament. By June of 1933, the German Evangelical churches had been substantially infiltrated and captured by this movement,[50] and, when one of their numbers, Ludwig Müller, was made head of the Protestant churches, the swastika flag of nazism flew from houses of worship throughout the nation.

Adolf Hitler knew that in order for his program to succeed, he would have to "deal" with the churches, either by unifying them with the Nazi ideology or disarming their power. Here is where we encounter the most important matter of the church's witness. Although much has been said and written, and with good justification, concerning the church's weak and belated response to nazism, it must also be noted that if Adolf Hitler had any trouble at all in bending the society of Germany to his will, it was encountered in relation to the Christian churches and their ministers, priests, and laity. They constituted, as Joachim Remak observes, "the one area where both propaganda and the state that meant to be total found their limits."[51]

To the church struggle, then, we now turn.

IV

Following World War II and the awful revelation of
Nazi crimes against Jews and other populations, the question naturally arose: Where was the church? Where was its
voice? Given the extent of Nazi destruction, by the government of a nation dotted with Christian churches, is there
not a sense in which Christians must share the guilt of the
Holocaust? These questions remain in the present day.

The subtleties and complexities of the "church struggle"
are beyond the scope of this discussion, but a general
context of understanding can be set in place. Those who
love to fault Christianity will, of course, find much ammu-
nition in various postwar laments and sorrowful appraisals
by German clergy. It was not the church's finest hour, and
all are agreed to that. Yet, as the only institution that did
not totally bend and succumb, the church witness must
have something positive to say to us. We also ought to
bear in mind a conclusion stated by Richard Gutteridge:

> Criticism or condemnation on our part, living as we
> did then, and do now, in a remarkably free and demo-
> cratic society, need to be tempered by the sober and
> honest self-inquiry as to whether we are certain that
> we could have done better, if as well, in the same
> circumstances. As Hitler fell, C.E.M. Joad . . . asked,
> "I wonder how many of those who criticize the Ger-
> mans for ignorance or docility or condemn them for
> positive complicity would have raised their voices
> against the government in their own country, had they
> known that death or torture were the penalties of
> criticism?"[52]

What is most incredible for us to grasp is that the
great majority of Christians in Germany either welcomed
Hitler to power or at least remained passively accepting of
his rule. In understanding this, a word must be said of the
historic relationships of church to state in Germany, Catholic as well as Protestant.

The Prussian Constitution of 1850 had brought considerable organizational liberties to churches, allowing them

to regulate their own affairs while remaining subject to the general laws of the state. Church-state relations were sometimes tense, as seen in the *Kulterkampf* (church and state struggle) of the 1870s and 1880s. This was a conflict between the Catholic church and the government that centered on state inspection of schools and requirements for state notification of appointment of clergy. Nevertheless, Catholicism gained considerable strength in Germany during the nineteenth century, and, in 1915, the church was free to own property, receive gifts and inheritances, and received direct governmental subsidies for educational programs. Ernst Helmreich observes that "the old fear that Catholicism was a minority religion in danger of being overwhelmed by a Protestant majority no longer haunted the church. It had achieved a standing throughout Germany such as it had not known since the days before the Reformation."[53]

As for the German Evangelical church, a long tradition of obedience to authority going all the way back to Luther was firmly in place. Historically, Lutheranism was keyed to monarchical and aristocratic systems of government. Most of the Lutheran clergy, it must be noted, were generally opposed to the unsuccessful attempt at democracy during the years of the Weimar Republic following World War I (1919–33). Beyond that, however, the Evangelical church had accepted many of the philosophic currents described previously. Since the early nineteenth century, the German Evangelical churches had developed a strong relationship between faith and state authority. Although some of this might be attributed to Martin Luther's views on obedience to the ruling authorities, Hegelian ideas were certainly involved as well. Patriotism flowered under the protection of religion, and the purposes of God had gradually become dangerously confused with national destiny, with the result of the creation of a national Protestant church. Historian Richard V. Pierard has clarified the implications of this development:

> God in Lutheran parlance became less the tender, loving Redeemer and more the God who leads his

people to victory. . . . The highest place in the divine
structure of creation was occupied by the *Völk* and its
concrete political form, the nation. The struggle for
the *Völkstum* became a struggle for God's order, indeed, for God himself. Service for *Völk* and fatherland
consequently was God's service, and devotion to the
community was the highest moral demand placed upon
an individual. Naturally, the deity was seen as the
German God and the people were his elect. His revelation was worked out in German history which meant
that political unity, monarchical power, and freedom
within a structure of authority were the fulfillment of
the divine dictates. The Reformation stress on the
justifying power of faith was supplanted by the proclamation of the nationality and its God, and national
mission became the new gospel.[54]

The further away from biblical authority the church
moved, the more vulnerable it was to the distortion which
equated Christian faith with German culture. One can see
the seeds of future tragedy in the thinking of prominent
theologians of the early twentieth century. Having adopted
the conclusions of the higher critics that there could be no
"once for all" revelation, they opted for the Hegelian concept of a salvation of historical process, with that process
now seen as raising up German culture as a redemptive
principle for humanity. When the first world war broke
out in 1914, many of these theologians supported the
aggressive policies of Kaiser Wilhelm II on the premise
that German culture must be preserved above all other
things. Adolf Harnack, perhaps Germany's leading theologian and biblical scholar at the turn of the century, stated
the belief that German culture "is the most precious possession of humanity . . . and we will pledge our wealth and
our blood to the last drop for this *Kulter*."[55] In a similar
vein, ninety-three German intellectuals signed a petition in
which such events as the killing of Belgian civilians and the
destruction of the library of Louvain were endorsed.
Harnack was among the signers, along with other theologians. By the time that Hitler came to power, all the pre-
cedents had been set and all the philosophic principles

established whereby a nationalistic idolatry could be sub-stituted for the gospel of Jesus Christ. William Hordern has noted that "for a century theologians had tried to modernize the faith by accommodating it to the modern age. Now, in Germany, Hitler was the modern age and thus it seemed logical to accommodate Christianity to this latest form of modernity."[56]

Hitler fulfilled the vision of the Völkish faith. He spoke of the unity of all Germans as "one blood," and his strength of leadership embodied the Führer principle. Also, his career, as presented in *Mein Kampf*, expressed the Nietzschean elements of spiritual struggle and a heroic vocation of cultural renewal. Although he proclaimed a "Positive Christianity," what he espoused bore no relation-ship to the biblical faith or to the Reformation theology of Luther. The heroic aggressiveness, anti-Semitism, and Germanic messianism of the Völkish faith all came to a meeting point in his person and work.

Nazism arrived with the full trappings of a full-blown religion. Nazi rallies were glorious pageants that stirred the emotions, which, according to Schleiermacher, were the very well-springs of spiritual truth. The faith to which Hitler called the German people depended not on any revelation of Scripture, but on pure feeling. The Nazi mixture of flags, rich and heroic music (especially that of the fanatically anti-Semitic genius Richard Wagner), and the message of national destiny had the effect of religious festivals. Even today, still photographs of these meetings have a powerful and gripping presence, and one can imag-ine the great impact that such a piece of cinematic propa-ganda as *Triumph of the Will* must have had through its showings in German theaters (see chapter 5).

The Völkish concept of the social organism was effec-tively symbolized in mass meetings that expressed a sense of eternity, awe, and mystery, effects stimulated by "cathe-dral of light" nighttime mass meetings in which antiair-craft lights sent brilliant shafts of illumination into the darkened sky. In his speeches, Hitler would frequently characterize his career in politics as a divine calling led by God and insisted that nazism was more than just a social

movement. It was a total worldview, a spirituality, supported by an energetic use of traditional religious words
that had, however, become detached from their orthodox,
historic meanings. His references to a "thousand year
Reich" carried the ring of the biblical millennium. "Essentially," writes historian Paul Johnson, "Nazism . . . was not
materialist; it was a blasphemous parody of Christianity,
with racialism substituted for God, and German 'blood'
for Christ." His description of this false religion illustrates
the Nazi genius for synthesizing and transforming familiar
religious practices, employing such things as feast days,
sacraments (such as special wedding services), and baptismal services.

> At SS baptismal ceremonies, the room was decorated
> with a centre altar containing a photograph of Hitler
> and a copy of *Mein Kampf*, and on the walls were
> candles, Nazi flags, the Tree of Life and branches of
> young trees. There was music from Grieg's *Peer Gynt*
> (Morning), readings from *Mein Kampf* and other ele-
> ments of the Christian ceremony; but the celebrant
> was an SS officer and the service concluded with the
> hymn of loyalty to the SS.[57]

Most troubling and shocking of all to us who look
back on it was the transformation of prayers and hymns.
One recalls, for example, a scene in the 1978 television
series "Holocaust," in which a Nazi bureaucrat, just returned from his work at a concentration camp, enjoys
Christmas with his family, all sitting together singing "Silent Night." Such things actually happened in the Third
Reich culture and strike us as incredible. But, documentary films of the period clarify the transformation that had
been taking place and show Christmas trees topped off *not*
with traditional "star-of-Bethlehem" decorations, but with
glowing swastikas. We also know that such hymns had
been given new words. Here is the Nazi version of "Silent
Night":

> Silent Night, holy night,
>
> All is calm, all is bright,

Only the Chancellor steadfast in fight,

Watches o'er Germany by day and night,

Always caring for us.[58]

Children were taught to pray in the name of Adolf Hitler.

Adolf Hitler, you are our great leader. Thy name makes the enemy tremble. Thy Third Reich comes, thy will alone is law upon earth. Let us hear daily thy voice and order us by thy leadership, for we will obey to the end even with our lives. We praise thee! Heil Hitler!

Führer, my Führer, sent to me from God, protect and maintain me throughout my life. Thou who hast saved Germany from deepest need, I thank thee today for my daily bread. Remain at my side and never leave me, Führer, my Führer, my faith, my light. Heil my Führer.[59]

The one great enemy of the Nazis was a deeply rooted, biblically based Christianity, or any form of historical orthodoxy, Catholic or Protestant, and proximity to these norms fueled what resistance the churches put up. Although resistance was slow in coming and limited in its application, it did occur. And, to the extent that it did, Christians of today may find instruction in the story.

The story of the Church struggle and how it has been reported is something of a story in itself. Two viewpoints can be found in the literature. The first and most familiar is the viewpoint expressed by Paul Johnson in *A History of Christianity*, in which the churches are seen as doing next to nothing, with what they did do understood as insignificant and always compromised by cowardice. Another view, however, is given by Franklin Littell in *The German Phoenix* in which he argues that the story of the resistance is really much deeper than most non-Europeans imagine and that the media reported very little on it, both in the postwar and wartime periods. Whatever the case may be, however, it is important to note the basis of the resistance that did, in fact, take place and to understand that "the Nazi campaign against the Churches was part of a wider process in which the banner of anti-clericalism was raised from one end of Europe to the other as a justification for violent repression carried out in the name of progress," and that "the Nazi campaign would never have achieved the success it did if the estrangement of millions from the faith of the Church had not already revealed a fatal weakening of Christianity."[60]

The Christians of Germany had begun to take serious notice of the Nazi party in 1930, the year in which the Nazis showed significant electoral power, and in which Rosenberg had published his *The Myth of the Twentieth Century*, an openly anti-Christian book that Hitler, in his desire to deceive the churches, publicly shunned. The churches should have known better, however, as Hitler appointed Rosenberg to head the spiritual and political education of Nazi party members. Indeed, some were discerning. A good number of Catholic theologians noticed early on, in the thirties, the clear incompatibility between Christian faith and the "positive Christianity" of nazism. In some dioceses, Catholics were forbidden to join the party, and, on New Year's Day, 1931, Cardinal Bertram of Breslau gave a prophetic warning against extreme nationalism, glorification of race, and "the vain imaginings of a national religious society" guided by "the racial theories of an Aryan-heathen teaching about salvation."[61] There was also Michael von Faulhaber, cardinal archbishop of Munich, who, during the Advent season of 1933, gave a series of sermons on "The Jewish, the Christian, and the Germanic." The sermons praised the Old Testament Hebrews who had given to human culture and to Christianity itself "the sublime and pure idea of God," and set forth clearly the connection between Christianity and Judaism. Quoting a fellow churchman, Faulhaber declared: "Cardinal Manning once said to the Jews: 'I would not understand my own religion did I not honor yours.'" He went on to warn his congregation (which consisted of overflow crowds) of a coming paganism in Germany that would seek to replace Christian traditions with Teutonic paganism, and expressed the hope that "the German nation will not betray and deny its Saviour that quickly."[62] A particularly courageous sermon was delivered by the bishop of Münster, Clemens Count Galen, on 13 July 1941—courageous because it crossed over the line from purely spiritual matters to comment on activities in the political sphere. Galen took on the actions of the Gestapo, Hitler's secret police organization. He pounded the state policies on the issue of justice and gave specific mention to particular measures—expulsion and arrest, imprisonment of fellow Germans in concentration camps, and the total lack of accountability of the secret police.[63]

There was also scholarly activity brought to bear in an attempt to refute Rosenberg's *Myth*. In 1934, the diocese of Münster issued *Studies in the Myth of the Twentieth Century*. This work attempted to show Rosenberg's defective scholarship in historical matters and refute his criticism of the Bible. Moreover, in 1938, the Sacred Congregation of Seminaries and Universities sent a letter to all dependent institutions urging teachers "to arm themselves from Biology, Philosophy, Apologetics, and the juridical moral disciplines to reject validly and learnedly" doctrines characteristic of nazism and fascism.[64]

Although significant numbers of Catholics were taken up in the spirit of national renewal embodied in Hitler, during the prewar years the church maintained an official attitude of reserve towards the National Socialist movement. Catholic doctrines were not affected by nazism, but Catholic society was shaken severely by the signing of the infamous concordat with the Vatican in the summer of 1933. This agreement, for which Pope Pius XI is ignominiously remembered, confined the actions of the church to merely "spiritual" matters, excluding it from the realm of politics. It had the effect of stripping the Catholic church of any cultural influence, an influence it had won through persistence and open conflict with the German state in the nineteenth century. Many have held, on the evidence of this concordat, that the Vatican, or Pius XI, was pro-fascist. This view overlooks some important history, however. Pius, no doubt, was hoping that Hitler would fulfill his public pledges made on 23 March 1933 to respect the rights of the churches. However, as Hitler's belligerence toward the church increased, Pius issued an encyclical, *Mit Brennender Sorge* (With Deep Anxiety) on 14 March 1937, which expressed an open condemnation of nazism. The message, which was read from all Catholic pulpits in Germany, places responsibility for growing tensions between church and state clearly in the Nazi corner and pointedly condemns the spiritual worldview and theological distortions of national socialism.

> He who, in pantheistic vagueness, equates God with the universe, and identifies God with the world and the world with God does not belong to believers in God. He who replaces a personal God with a weird impersonal Fate supposedly according to ancient pre-Christian German concepts denies the wisdom and providence of God. . . . You must be especially alert, Venerable Brethren, when fundamental religious conceptions are robbed of their intrinsic content and made to mean something else in a profane sense.

The encyclical defines the reality of sin in the human race and exalts Jesus Christ as the one and true Savior. It concludes with a ringing exhortation that persecution will only advance the purification and spiritual strength of the church, to the ultimate victory of Jesus.

> Then—of this We are certain—will the enemies of the Church, who fancy that her hour has come, soon recognize that they rejoiced too soon and were too quick to dig her grave. Then will the day come when, instead of the too hasty songs of victory raised by the enemies of Christ, the *Te Deum* of liberation can rise to heaven from the hearts and lips of Christ's faithful; a *Te Deum* of thanks to the Highest; a *Te Deum* of joy, that the German people, even in its erring sons of today, has trodden the way of religious homecoming, that they once more bend the knee in faith purified by suffering before the King of time and eternity, Jesus Christ, and that they prepare to fulfill that calling which the designs of the Eternal God point out to

them, in the struggle against the deniers and destroyers of the Christian west, in harmony with all right-minded people of other nations.[65]

It is also known that Pius battled the fascist regime of Mussolini in Italy and, as early as 1926, condemned fascist movements in France. "Increasingly distressed by Hitler's and Mussolini's treatment of the Church and by their vicious racist policies, Pius was preparing an explosive encyclical denouncing Fascist crimes and racism when he was overtaken by death on February 10, 1939."[66]

The concordat was a great tragedy, however, because the one thing Hitler genuinely feared was a real struggle with the churches. Although Hitler had rejected his own Catholic upbringing, he had a form of respect for the church as an institution. After all, any organization that had managed to maintain its existence and power for two thousand years was, potentially, a formidable enemy. With great care, cleverness, and deceit, Hitler was able to turn the church's good instincts against itself—inclinations toward a cooperative stance that might have positive effects on national regeneration as well as potential for the ongoing ministry of the church's various programs.

The Catholics had reservations about Hitler, and with good reason. Not only was there his connection with Rosenberg, but the suspicions of the church were amply aroused by evidences of Nazi hostility in the form of searches carried out in priests' homes and the dismissal of Catholic civil servants. Moreover, some Catholic properties were seized, papers censored, and schools closed, all prior to the concordat. In March 1933, Cardinal Bertram had made it clear to Vice Chancellor von Papen that the church could, indeed, sustain a drawn out opposition to the Nazi state, citing "errors of doctrine," "hostile character," and "desired totality of power" as issues of contention. Hitler was able to disarm these concerns in a speech to the Reichstag on 23 March 1933 in which he seemed to give assurances to Christianity, Catholic and Protestant, that "it was the most important factor for the maintenance of society." He spoke of "the sincere cooperation between

Church and State" and the Christian churches' "due influence in schools and education." As for Catholicism specifically, Hitler expressed concern for "the cultivation and maintenance of the friendliest relations with the Holy See" and promised outright that "the rights of the churches will not be curtailed."[67]

It meant nothing at all, but it served to dilute Catholic concerns, and the concordat was eventually signed on the urging of the German bishops in the belief that the status of the church in Germany would be respected. However, the outcome was disastrous inasmuch as the concordat limited church activities to merely religious functions, stripping it of any legitimate initiatives in the secular sphere. In one stroke, Hitler had effectively stripped German Catholicism of any power in the political and social spheres while at the same time establishing diplomatic legitimacy for the Nazi revolution. The church accepted the disbanding of all organizations that were not purely "spiritual"— its trade unions, political parties, and even discussion groups. Paul Johnson writes of this, that "the surrender was amazing; a century of German Catholic social activity was scrapped without a fight."[68]

The Evangelical (Protestant) churches, in contrast to Catholic apprehensions, were openly enthusiastic about Hitler and the Nazi party, seeing in the movement the hopes of a restored national church. As early as the 1920s, some churches had formed the Federation For a German Church, which had the dual goals of expunging Jewish elements from Christianity and fostering a national religion rooted in Germanic traditions. Later, the Thuringian German Christians formed out of a spirit that sought to remove from the church the limitations of outmoded orthodoxies and bureaucracies, while advocating a completely new interpretation of the faith for a new age. For them, a new revelation had come in Adolf Hitler. A third group, the "Christian German movement," sought to engage the Lutheran churches in political action and supplied chaplains to the Nazi paramilitary organization, the SA. These three factions unified in 1932 to form the "Faith movement of German Christians."

The bizarre thinking of this movement is reflected in a statement issued by the Thuringian pastors, 11 December 1933. In a "Directive of the Church" they stated that, while believing in Jesus Christ, in the power of his cross and resurrection, God's creation had nevertheless placed them "in the community of blood and fate of the German people." As such, they held themselves, as Christians, to be "responsible for the nation's future." The fusing of Christian mission with national destiny was implied in their bold statement, "Germany is our task, Christ is our strength." Claiming "the divine revelation of scripture" as the "source and confirmation of our faith," they also set forth the claim that there is a divine law created especially by God that was peculiar to the German nation itself. This "law" of God "took shape in the Leader Adolf Hitler, and in the National Socialist state created by him. This law speaks to us from the history of our people, a history grown of blood and soil. It is loyalty to this law which demands of us the battle for honor and freedom." The idolatrous character of this declaration is clearly revealed in the tone of the fourth article, where these pastors state that Jesus Christ reigns in grace and forgiveness in the faithful German congregation, and that "from this community of German Christians there shall grow a 'German Christian national Church,' embracing the entire people in the National Socialist state of Adolf Hitler. One Nation! One God! One Reich! One Church!"[69]

The extent of the German Christians' theological confusion is also seen in a catechism for "Positive Christianity" authored by the German professor Ernst Bergmann. In 1934, Bergmann summarized essential points of German religion. It was a religion "without dogma," revealed on a natural level within the human mentality. Man, according to Bergmann, "is the birthplace of God," and he dismisses traditional Christian concepts of sin, guilt, and repentance as "artificially engendered complexes in man." The proper German religion is grounded in heroism, courage, and chivalry and has nothing to do with grace, or the forgiveness of sin. "Anyone who is inclined to forgive sin," he wrote, "in reality sanctions sin. The act of forgiveness of sin really undermines religious ethics and tends to destroy the morale of the people."[70]

Understandably, Hitler saw in such people and statements useful allies. And, the Catholics might be forgiven if they saw some dangers to themselves. For a time, Hitler gave the German Christian movement quiet support, although his aim was merely to disrupt and eventually disarm any trouble that might come from the Protestants as well as the Catholics. Hitler held the Protestant clergy in deepest scorn, remarking once to Rosenberg that they would do anything to keep their jobs and comforts. That this attitude extended in the direction of the German Christians is seen in his later abandonment of them in the recognition that they constituted a rival movement within the overall Nazi movement. Besides, Hitler didn't want Christianity in any form linked to the political sphere. There is little doubt that Hitler's ultimate goal was the final destruction of the Jews and Christianity alike. Any form of national church was inimical to that task.

Yet, in Protestant churches as in Catholic churches, there were those who opposed the Nazi worldview and program, whose recognition of nazism as evil was rooted, as J.S. Conway observes, in their unceasing "appeal to the foundations of Christian teaching."[71] Indeed, such people understood the root issue—idolatry—a competition of absolutes. Similarly, Herbert Stroup recommends the thesis of Franklin H. Littell that the capacity of churches and individual Christians to resist national socialism, while undermined by the liberal and secularized versions of Christianity, was fueled specifically by elements that were narrowly churchly and theological.[72]

Resistance in the Protestant churches was stimulated by the National Synod of the German Lutheran churches in September of 1933. At this meeting, Pastor Julius Leutheuser, a leader of the Thuringian movement, had declared nothing less than the identification of the goals of nazism with the tenets of Christianity and that Christ had come to Germany through Adolf Hitler. Additional stimulus to spiritual discernment came through the attempts of the Nazi party to have the church introduce an

"Aryan paragraph" to its confession of faith, thereby making it illegal for a Jew to join the Christian church. Alarmed, the Berlin pastor Martin Niemöller circulated a letter to pastors encouraging them to join a "Pastor's Emergency League" for purposes of committing themselves "to be bound only by Holy Scripture and the Confessions of the Reformation."[73] This movement eventually led to the "Confessing Church," which emphasized the importance of doctrinal affirmation and which challenged the ideological drift of the German Christians. The first synod meeting of the association was held at Barmen on 29 May 1934, and the foundations for the Confessing Church were put in place there. The pastors issued a six-point statement, now known as the Barmen Confession. Each article was preceded with a scriptural reference, followed by a statement of what the synod affirmed and rejected. The Barmen Confession is notable for its clear affirmation that "Jesus Christ as he is attested for us in Holy Scripture is the one Word of God" and for its denial of legitimacy to the State as the single and totalitarian order of human life. In 1935, the Confessionals published a statement at their second synod, held at Pastor Niemöller's Berlin-Dahlem church, that constituted nothing less than a frontal attack on the ideology of nazism, and, in the assessment of Joachim Remak, it remains "one of the great basic documents of the Christian conscience under a modern dictatorship."[74] In *Appeal of the Second Confessing Synod of the Evangelical Church of the Old Prussian Union*, the Confessing pastors expressed the view that the German people were threatened by a mortal danger—the new religion of nazism, which constituted an idolatrous violation of the first commandment. It was nothing less than rebellion against God. The new faith was condemned on three major points:

> 1. In it, the racial and folkish ideology becomes a myth. In it, blood and race, nationality, honor, and freedom become idols.
>
> 2. The faith in an "eternal Germany" demanded by this religion replaces the faith in the eternal kingdom of our Lord and Saviour Jesus Christ.

3. This false faith creates its god in man's image and essence. In it, man honors, justifies, and redeems himself. Such idolatry has nothing in common with positive Christianity. It is the expression of the Antichrist.[75]

By the end of 1933, the Pastor's Emergency League had attracted almost one-third of Germany's Protestant clergymen, but the organization was never fully unified or able to make much of an impact. Various reasons underlie this fragmentation. In the first place, many of the pastors could not shake the traditional Lutheran call to obedience to the authorities. Today, as we look back with hindsight, we think naturally of massive civil disobedience as a way of protesting injustice. What we cannot fathom, though, is that the church in Germany had absolutely no tradition, theological or cultural, upon which to form a rationale for conflict with the state. In view of this, the statement of the Confessing Church quoted above seems all the more courageous and radical. Beyond such factors, however, was the unprecedented cleverness with which the National Socialists acted in relation to the churches, uttering statements of conciliation while at the same time exerting various pressures or acts of violence against them. It was actually the case that some churchmen saw the acts of antagonism as the mere products of a "radical wing" within the Nazi party that did not actually reflect Hitler's own goals. So, they continued to hope that positive relations could be worked out. In actuality, the whole situation was unprecedented for them. The same cannot be said for us today.

Still, there should have been no ambiguity of Christian conscience after 9 November 1938. On that night, the Nazis launched the pogrom known as "Crystal Night," in which party gangs assaulted Jewish people and property in an outpouring of destruction. It was the beginning of what eventually came to be conceived as "the final solution" to the Jewish presence in Germany and throughout Europe. There were protests in the form of statements and letters, and sometimes personal interviews with political leaders, but such action assumed what was no longer true—that the leaders of the nation were rational and responsible human beings who might be persuaded by argument. The real question, which apparently never took hold in the Confessing Church as a whole, was expressed by a church member in Breslau, Frau Annemarie Viebig, in her diary entry of November 9: "Are we still living in a State that can in any way be called righteous or civilized, rational or humane?"[76]

We must not assume, however, that nothing was accomplished by Christians by way of opposition to the regime or by way of aiding the persecuted, most notably the Jews. Birgir Forrell, in a postwar assessment of the resistance, affirmed that

> the number of Protestants, lay or ecclesiastical, who courageously put up a firm resistance to the National-Socialist regime before and during the war is not so small as is usually thought abroad. For the eminent ecclesiastical figures . . . are not the only ones to have taken the risks of a personal stand. In many communities violent incidents took place, and obscure Protestants took great risks and made great sacrifices to uphold their Christian ideas.[77]

This assessment is corroborated by a 1941 statement of the Nazi Martin Bormann, who declared the outright incompatibility of Christian and National Socialist views and complained that both churches of Germany, Catholic and Protestant, stood in the way of nazism with equal hostility.

Generally, critics of the church's performance give no indication of this. If it is recognized at all, it is usually accompanied by the charge that the churches were merely concerned with maintaining their own privileges, their own sphere of authority. But, even if but one single pastor, priest, or layperson paid a price out of love for Jesus Christ and the Word of God, the act would have to be acknowledged and remembered. In fact, there were many more than one, as we will see in chapter 4. For us, today, should we focus not merely on what or who failed, but also on what was accomplished, and why? Perhaps when we do, we will grasp with greater depth how it was that, in the context of greatest tyranny, it was possible yet to discover the limitations of evil and the eternity of Truth.

Endnotes

1. George Santayana, *Winds of Doctrine* (London: J.M. Dent and Sons, Ltd., 1913), 1.

2. Michael Harrington, *The Politics at God's Funeral* (New York: Holt, Rinehart and Winston, 1983), 174-75.

3. Robert Waite, *The Psychopathic God: Adolf Hitler* (New York: Basic Books, 1977), 271.

4. Robert Nisbet, *History of the Idea of Progress* (New York: Basic Books, 1980), 278-82.

5. Leonard Peikoff, *The Ominous Parallels: The End of Freedom in America* (New York: New American Library, 1982), 35.

6. Heinz Lubasz, ed., *Fascism: Three Major Regimes* (New York: John Wiley and Sons, Inc., 1973), 40.

7. Nisbet, *History of the Idea of Progress*, 277.

8. Fritz Stern, *The Politics of Cultural Despair: A Study in the Rise of the German Ideology* (Berkeley and Los Angeles: University of California Press, 1961), 285.

9. William Hubben, *Dostoyevsky, Kierkegaard, Nietzsche, and Kafka: Four Apostles of Our Destiny* (New York: Collier Books, 1962), 124.

10. Erich Kahler, *Man the Measure* (Cleveland: World Publishing Company, 1943, 1967), 582.

11. Walter Kaufmann, *The Portable Nietzsche* (New York: The Viking Press, 1954), 570-72.

12. Wilhelm Grenzmann, "Nietzsche and National Socialism" in *The Third Reich*, ed. Jacques Rueff (New York: Frederick A. Praeger, 1955), 221.

13. Kahler, *Man the Measure* 584-87.

14. Ibid.

15. Dennis Prager and Joseph Telushkin, *Why the Jews?* (New York: Simon and Schuster, 1983), 20.

16. Hannah Arendt, *Antisemitism: Part One of the Origins of Totalitarianism* (New York: Harcourt, Brace and World, Inc., 1968), viii–ix.

17. Prager and Telushkin, *Why the Jews?*, 94–96.

18. Vamberto Morais, *A Short History of Antisemitism* (New York: W.W. Morton, 1976), 152.

19. Prager and Telushkin, *Why the Jews?*, 108.

20. Richard Gutteridge, *Open Thy Mouth for the Dumb* (Oxford: Basil Blackwell, 1976), 322.

21. H.H. Ben-Sasson, *A History of the Jewish People* (Cambridge, Massachusetts: Harvard University Press, 1976), 648–49.

22. Gutteridge, *Open Thy Mouth for the Dumb*, 318.

23. Arthur Hertzberg, *The French Enlightenment and the Jews* (New York: Columbia University Press, 1968), 10.

24. Ibid., 313.

25. Robert Proctor, *Racial Hygiene: Medicine under the Nazis* (Cambridge, Massachusetts: Harvard University Press, 1988), 13–14.

26. Joachim Remak, *The Nazi Years: A Documentary History* (New York: Simon and Schuster, 1969), 3–4.

27. Waite, *The Psychopathic God*, 261.

28. Nisbet, *History of the Idea of Progress*, 274.

29. Peter Viereck, *Metapolitics: The Roots of the Nazi Mind*, rev. ed. (New York: Capricorn Books, 1965), 18.

30. George L. Mosse, *The Crisis of German Ideology* (New York: Grosset and Dunlap, 1964), 14–19.

31. Ibid., 25.

32. Stern, *The Politics of Cultural Despair*, xiii,

33. Jean-Jacques Anstett, "Paul de Lagarde" in *The Third Reich*, 184.

34. Arthur A. Cohen, *The Myth of the Judeo-Christian Tradition* (New York: Harper and Row, 1970), 198.

35. Mosse, *The Crisis of German Ideology*, 43.

36. Stern, *The Politics of Cultural Despair*, 42.

37. Ibid., 63.

38. Ibid., 116–17.

39. Ibid., 118–19.

40. Ibid., 141.

41. Mosse, *The Crisis of German Ideology*, 45–46.

42. Ibid., 50.

43. Cohen, *The Myth of the Judeo-Christian Tradition*, 199.

44. Jean Real, "The Religious Conception of Race" in *The Third Reich*, 256.

45. Houston Stewart Chamberlain, *The Foundations of the Nineteenth Century*, trans. John Lees (New York: John Lane Company, 1910), 1:332.

46. Real, "The Religious Conception of Race," 281.

47. Ibid., 200–16.

48. Edmond Vermeil, "German Nationalist Ideology in 19th and 20th Centuries," in *The Third Reich*, 96.

49. Ibid., 97.

50. Konrad Heiden, *Der Feuhrer* (New York: Lexington Press, 1944), 638.

51. Remak, *The Nazi Years*, 94.

52. Gutteridge, *Open Thy Mouth for the Dumb*, 304–05.

53. Ernst Christian Helmreich, *The German Churches under Hitler* (Detroit: Wayne State University Press, 1979), 59–60.

54. Richard V. Pierard, "Why Did Protestants Welcome Hitler?" *Fides et Historia* (Spring, 1978): 8–9.

55. Daniel P. Fuller, *Easter Faith and History* (Grand Rapids, Michigan: William B. Eerdmans, 1965), 79.

56. William Hordern, *A Layman's Guide to Protestant Theology* (New York: Macmillian Company, 1968), 135.

57. Paul Johnson, *A History of Christianity* (New York: Atheneum, 1976), 486.

58. Ibid., 487.

59. Waite, *The Psychopathic God*, 31.

60. John S. Conway, *The Nazi Persecution of the Churches, 1933–45* (New York: Basic Books, 1968), 486.

61. Ibid., 6–7.

62. Remak, *The Nazi Years*, 98–99.

63. Ibid.

64. Albert R. Chandler, *Rosenberg's Nazi Myth* (New York: Cornell University, 1945), 107.

65. Louis L. Snyder, ed., *Hitler's Third Reich: A Documentary History* (Chicago: Nelson-Hall, Inc., 1981), 249–60.

66. Thomas Bokenkotter, *A Concise History of the Catholic Church* (New York: Doubleday and Company, Inc., 1979), 403–4.

67. Conway, *The Nazi Persecution*, 20.

68. Johnson, *A History of Christianity*, 483.

69. Remak, *The Nazi Years*, 95–96.

70. Snyder, *Hitler's Third Reich*, 167–69.

71. Conway, *The Nazi Persecution*, 46.

72. Herbert Stroup, *Church and State in Confrontation* (New York: The Seabury Press, 1967), 172–73.

73. Conway, *The Nazi Persecution*, 49.

74. Remak, *The Nazi Years*, 100.

75. Ibid.

76. Gutteridge, *Open Thy Mouth for the Dumb*, 178.

77. Birgir Forrell, "National Socialism and the Protestant Churches in Germany" in *The Third Reich*, 831.

$$\int \quad \text{TWO} \quad \int$$

Is the New Testament
Anti-Semitic?

One of the more aggressive accusations raised against the Bible in the post-Holocaust years is the charge that the New Testament itself contains the seeds of anti-Semitism. The problem is not seen merely as a matter of false interpretation, but as the communication of Jew hatred in the Scripture itself. In this view, the early Church developed anti-Semitic attitudes as a result of conflict with Jewish groups, and these attitudes are expressed in the New Testament documents. A Jerusalem rabbi, Eliezar Berkovits, has stated the view that the New Testament is "the most dangerous anti-Semitic tract in history," and according to the Christian historian Paul L. Maier, the rabbi's views are shared by a growing number of Christian theologians who would call for editorial exclusion of all such "anti-Semitic" passages from the Bible![1] According to authors Dennis Prager and Joseph Telushkin, the New Testament is largely an anti-Jewish polemic, which they suggest was written for the singular purpose of discrediting Israel. They view the founders of Christianity as promulgating arbitrary doctrines while attributing them to Jesus, doctrines which constitute the theological invalidation of the Jews' continuing existence. For them, the New Testament "canonized anti-Semitism."[2] Citing various New Testament sources of alleged anti-Semitism, Jewish scholar Samuel Sandmel has interpreted Jesus' denunciation of the Scribes and Pharisees in Matthew, chapter 23, as a polemic by the early Church against all Jews, thereby setting forth a particularly popular citation of "biblical" anti-Semitism.[3]

The issue of "Christian anti-Semitism," then, is raised in relation to the Holocaust not merely in reference to Church history, but in respect to the Christian Scriptures as well. It is a serious issue precisely because of the implicit discrediting of the New Testament as the Word of God. No doubt this approach to the problem of anti-Semitism is undertaken in many cases as a sincere effort to heal wounds and lay a foundation for Jewish-Christian understanding. There is also, however, a kind of "holocaust chic" that various intellectuals find helpful to the general discrediting of the Bible and Christian faith. The notion that Scripture itself contains a virus of hatred like anti-Semitism is all-too-convenient to their enterprise. Indeed, the charge of New Testament anti-Semitism updates the overall tendency of the post-Enlightenment world to hang every evil imaginable on the doorstep of the Christian faith. Nevertheless, the issue is important, for the implicit accusation is that the Bible contains such a faulty view of humanity that the hatred of the Nazis for the Jews was somehow the outgrowth of biblical religion and theological orthodoxy. Although Jewish writers like Sandmel and Richard Rubenstein (see chapter 3) do not actually affirm such a view, their work is often cited in support of the position, for both assert that the New Testament is a source of antagonism toward Jews as a collectivity.

The fundamental view is that the New Testament and anti-Semitism go hand in hand together. History, though, challenges this position. Whereas it is true that the Church visited much persecution upon the Jews during the Middle Ages, one could well argue that these actions were hardly the result of the Church's adherence to New Testament authority. The Medieval Church is not notable for a recognition of the centrality of Scripture, and, even if certain passages of the New Testament were quoted to support actions against the Jews, what does that prove? The question, always, is the validity of interpretation. In fact, the Church's forsaking of scriptural authority was the precise issue of the Protestant Reformation. We also do well to take note of the persecution of Christians—various proto-Reformation "heretics"—for their recognition of biblical authority over Church tradition or mere papal power. Jews and biblically orientated Christians alike were regarded as enemies or heretics, and, if one speaks of a Medieval "Christian" anti-Semitism, one might just as easily speak of a "Christian" anti-Christianity. An accurate assessment of "Christian anti-Semitism" recognizes that the historic persecution of Jews by the Church was one facet of a larger antagonism against all who resisted the authority of Rome.

Sandmel himself attributes the persecutions to the general propensity of mankind for cruelty. "The persecutions of Jews by Christians ought to be seen as one of the many horrors with which the history of mankind has been unduly filled, and it represents not so much a Christian characteristic as a human one."[4] He rejects the notion that nazism represented a "Christian" form of anti-Semitism, pointing out that such confusion can only come through mistakenly identifying "Gentile" with "Christian." Further, he makes it clear that the historic allegation that Jews, as a collectivity, are "Christ-killers" is not found in the New Testament.[5] Rather, he sees the Gospels as revealing more of a Roman motive for killing Jesus than a purely Jewish one. Prager and Telushkin do not see it this way, however, and hold that the editors of the New Testament went beyond a simple historical narrative of the Jewish opposition to Jesus and Jesus' Crucifixion to suggest that all Jews, then and forever, are implicated in the murder of Jesus and, therefore, God himself.[6] Sandmel observes, though, that Jewish blame for the Crucifixion is virtually absent from the Pauline Epistles, while making a possible exception in the case of 1 Thessalonians 2:15.[7]

In view of this, it is interesting to consider the impact of the Protestant Reformation upon Jewish-Christian relationships, for the Reformation was centered in the recognition of biblical authority as the key to Christian faith and practice. Although considerable anti-Jewish sentiment continued during and in the wake of the Reformation, measurable improvement did in fact occur, and such improvement can be traced to the growing respect for the Bible that the Reformation brought about.

H.H. Ben-Sasson, a leading scholar of the Hebrew University in Jerusalem, has written of the significance of the Christian reformation for Jewish history. In his monumental work, *A History of the Jewish People* (which he edited and partially wrote), Ben-Sasson notes that the Reformation benefited the Jews for two major reasons, one sociological and the other theological. Sociologically, the Reformation broke the unified authority of Christendom. Not only was there a basic Catholic-Protestant division, but there were various sects developing within Protestantism, making it impossible for any one of the churches to exert the kind of authority enjoyed by the Medieval Church. Jews, then, "ceased to be the only open non-conformists in the cities and kingdoms of Europe" and "dwelt side by side with Christians with differing views, which were mutually regarded as heretical."[8] These sectarian divisions and expressions of individualist views, observes Ben-Sasson, eventually undermined all tendencies toward religious compulsion and religious intolerance. But, the Protestant view of the Bible was also a major factor in changing the Jewish position in society. Because the Protestants turned to the Old and New Testaments alike for their ultimate authority and their search for a better social structure, "several Christian sects and leading Protestant thinkers [turned] back to the systems and aims of the Law as expressed in the Old Testament in the behavior of the judges, prophets and kings of Israel."[9] As a result, Hebrew Scripture and language became important social and political assets in Protestant culture.

Ben-Sasson notes that, although some Christians used the Bible to justify bad treatment of the Jews, "others, as a result of their studies of the Bible and of Hebrew, tended to respect the Jews, to take an interest in their way of life and to appreciate their past and its continuity," tendencies that led eventually to favorable conditions for Jews in the Netherlands and England.[10]

Significantly, Ben-Sasson regards Martin Luther's anti-Jewish polemics (see chapter 1) as being out of the mainstream of reformation trends. Luther's favorable view of the Jews expressed in 1523 contrasted markedly with the 1543 pamphlet *Against the Jews*. However, Ben-Sasson puts Luther in perspective, relative to the Reformation as a whole. Recognizing the viciousness of Luther's attack, he notes that the very vitality of the Reformation that Luther had led insured that most elements of the Lutheran world historically paid more attention to the Luther of 1523 than the aging Luther of 1543. Even during the time of Luther's anti-Jewish polemics, "his circle included those who maintained their friendly approach to the Jews more consistently and systematically than he did."[11]

Another Jewish scholar and contributor to *A History of the Jewish People* is Shmuel Ettinger, who writes of the impact of a growing biblical authority upon Jewish-Christian relations. Of conditions in the seventeenth century, Ettinger mentions the rising importance of Hebrew and Jewish literature in the spiritual life of Europe, which saw an increasing number of learned Christian Hebraists at European universities, as well as special chairs in Hebrew and Jewish studies. "The Bible became more important as an authority for political thought, and the society and state of ancient Israel were held up as an example of an enlightened political society."[12] By way of contrast, Ettinger notes the hostility of the French Enlightenment philosophers to the Bible, and the transmission of their negativism into Germany via Johann Fichte.

Historical inquiry reveals, then, a discernible pattern whereby a respect for the Bible by scholars and theologians worked to break down centuries-old tendencies toward anti-Semitism and anti-Judaism. This trend was itself broken, however, by the Enlightenment's scornful attack on the Bible and the tendency of the "higher critics" to

attribute the unique Jewish spiritual development to bor-
rowings from other cultures, thereby disparaging Jews and
Judaism. In fact, some of the scholars in the higher critical
tradition were openly anti-Semitic. Bruno Bauer, for example, who greatly influenced German higher criticism,
was a "vicious Jew-baiter" who opposed citizenship for
Jews in Germany,[13] and Gerhard Kittel, one of the foremost names in contemporary liberal scholarship, held that
"authentic Judaism" is characterized by the symbol of a
restless stranger, wandering and homeless in the earth.
Others, such as Walter Grundmann, sought to show that
Jesus was psychologically, biologically, and physically un-
Jewish, a view also affirmed by Martin Dibelius.[14]

It does not seem, then, that regard for the inspiration
and authority of the Bible as the Word of God encourages
anti-Semitism. The pattern seems to be the opposite, and
it must be acknowledged, with some emphasis, that the
Holocaust took place in a century of great skepticism toward biblical authority, especially among the intellectual
classes.

But, the question remains as to whether there is substance to the suggestion that the New Testament contains
actual elements of anti-Semitism as suggested by various
writers. Certainly, no person can read the New Testament
without identifying a Christian tension with Judaism, but
does this tension justify the notion that the Christians'
primary source documents are in fact anti-Semitic?

The refutation of this claim comes through reading
the New Testament itself. When we do so, we find that any
basis for a racist posture is unavailable. The tone of the
New Testament teaching is brought out in various places.
I will concentrate on those sources that seem most perti-
nent to the issue, these being the Pauline Epistles, the
Book of Hebrews, chapter 8 of the Gospel of John, and
Matthew, chapter 23.

Paul's Epistle to the Romans is the most comprehensive presentation of the plan of salvation in the New Testament. In this epistle, Paul sets forth the nature of sin
and its consequences, the role of faith, as well as instruc-

tions in regard to Christian conduct. He also has something to say in regard to the Jews, of whom he was one. He writes that the gospel "is the power of God for salvation to every one who has faith, to the Jew first and also to the Greek" (Rom. 1:16). This is echoed further on in the epistle when he writes: "There will be tribulation and distress for every human being who does evil, the Jew first and also the Greek, but glory and honor and peace for every one who does good, the Jew first and also the Greek" (Rom. 2:9–10). What is the point? Clearly, that God does not save people or endow them with spiritual status on the basis of race or national origin! Jew and Gentile alike are saved through faith in the gospel. This gospel was first preached to the people of Israel, as the synoptic Gospels indicate, because they had been prepared for the revelation of the Redeemer through centuries of prophecy (Luke 1:67–80). This was the "advantage"—that "the Jews are entrusted with the oracles of God" (Rom. 3:1–2). However, this did not mean that the Jews were better or worse, as people, than the Gentiles. "What then? Are the Jews better off? No, not at all; for I have already charged that all men, both Jews and Greeks, are under the power of sin, as it is written: 'None is righteous, no, not one'" (Rom. 3:9).

By the time Paul wrote the Epistle to the Romans, there had been considerable division between adherents to Judaism and the emergent Christian faith. It is interesting to speculate as to the reasons for the Jewish rejection of Christ and their resentment toward the gospel. It is quite possible that there was more to it than just religious understandings. For centuries, the Jews had regarded the Gentile peoples with scorn, apparently forgetting the Old Testament commandment that God had called them to be a light to the nations. The inclusion of Gentiles into the Body of Christ must have been a severe barrier to many in the Jewish theological establishment, just as it had been a problem for the first Christians, who were Jews themselves and who at first did not understand the universal implications of Jesus' death and resurrection for all (see

Acts, chapter 10). However, the Jewish rejection of the gospel does not occasion hatred in Paul, but rather a loving anguish that they too might know the Saviour:

> I am speaking the truth in Christ, I am not lying; my conscience bears me witness in the Holy Spirit, that I have great sorrow and unceasing anguish in my heart. For I could wish that I myself were accursed and cut off from Christ for the sake of my brethren, my kinsmen by race. They are Israelites, and to them belong the sonship, the glory, the covenants, the giving of the law, the worship, and the promises; to them belong the patriarchs, and of their race, according to the flesh, is the Christ. (Rom. 9:1–5)

In view of such remarks, one might well understand the Nazis finding the Bible to be offensive, and why "Pauline" Christianity had to be discredited. Elsewhere, the apostle had declared to a meeting of Gentiles in Athens that God had made of "one blood" all the nations of the earth (Acts 17:26). There could not be much comfort for a Houston Stewart Chamberlain in such a proclamation.

Yet, there is the problem of 1 Thessalonians 2:15. This verse, taken by itself, indicates that the Jews "killed both the Lord Jesus and the prophets, and drove us out, and displease God and oppose all men." A shallow consideration of this verse, isolated from its context, might indeed serve an anti-Semitic polemic, but when it is considered in terms of its immediate context as well as the general context of Paul's writing, no such conclusion seems valid. Paul was writing to a church of converted pagans who were undergoing persecution and scorn from the majority in Thessalonica, who kept to the old religious cult practices surrounding the classical gods. He wanted them to understand that their situation paralleled that of the Christian brethren in Judea, relative to Jews who opposed the gospel. This is made clear in verse 14: "For you, brethren, became imitators of the churches of God in Christ Jesus which are in Judea; for you suffered the same things from your own countrymen as they did from the Jews." Paul is indicating that God's redeeming act in Christ is opposed by all, Jew and Gentile alike. It is true that Paul refers to "the Jews, who killed . . . the Lord Jesus and the prophets" (1 Thess. 2:15). However, he also says that the Thessalonians suffer "the same things." The attitude of the Gentiles who are persecuting the Thessalonian believers is paralleled to the attitudes and acts of those who sought the death of Jesus. If there is any "Christ-killer" implication in this passage, it would seem to extend to Jew and Gentile both, not just the Jews. Further, when Paul writes that the Jews killed the prophets, he is not saying anything that was not already admitted in Jewish literature itself.

Next, we consider the Book of Hebrews. This book constitutes an apologetic for the sufficiency of Jesus Christ as Savior and Lord, and it seems to have been written to a body of Jewish Christians. It is heavily touched with references to Jewish religious practices and Old Testament people of faith. The intent of the author is to show how Christ fulfills the faith of Judaism. In this book, one is able to see how Judaism preceded and foreshadowed the ministry of Jesus Christ and how dependent the Christian revelation is upon the Old Testament faith. A "Christianity" without Jewish roots is impossible! Yet, Christ supersedes the Old Testament prophets, practices, and heroes of faith. "In many and various ways God spoke of old to our fathers by the prophets; but in these last days he has spoken to us by a Son, whom he appointed the heir of all things, through whom also he created the world" (Heb. 1:1). The Son of God himself is now the high priest of the faithful; he was slain for the sins of mankind and is raised from the dead. Of what continuing value, then, is the blood of animal sacrifices and the intercession of temple priests? Christ's claim to have come in fulfillment of the Law (Matt. 5:17–18) is true, and, for this reason, those who believe in him may "with confidence draw near to the throne of grace" (Heb. 4:16).

In Hebrews, the present ministry of Christ is presented in Jewish terms throughout. The author, while stressing the superiority of Christ over all and the passing away of the old sacrificial temple system, does not insult Judaism. Rather, Judaism is presented as the necessary foreshadowing of God's finished work of salvation through Christ. The priesthood of Christ, which is the dominant theme in Hebrews, is inseparably linked to Jewish religious understanding. Again, such Jewishness to the Christian faith affords no comfort for those who would seek a biblical base for anti-Semitism. If anything provided a base for a "Christian anti-Semitism" among the Nazis, it was more likely the thinking of such liberal theologians and scholars as Ernst Renan and Adolf Harnack. Renan, employing Hegel's concept of "absolute spirit," separated Jesus from his Jewish background, seeming to set Jesus over and against Judaism as an "ideal man," while Harnack ruled out all doctrine and even denied Jesus had any rabbinical background. For Samuel Sandmel, the work of these scholars represents "the extreme in capricious selection and exclusion."[15]

Finally, there are the Gospels themselves, and most efforts to associate an anti-Semitic message with the biblical literature center on John, chapter 8, and Matthew, chapter 23.

In chapter 8 of John, we find the following words of Jesus addressed to "the Jews": "You are of your father the devil, and your will is to do your father's desires" (v. 44). Sandmel writes of the Gospel of John that "in its utility for later Jew-haters, the Fourth Gospel is pre-eminent among the New Testament writings."[16] One must admit that if a person were looking for a biblical base for anti-Semitism, this verse might be the key, provided he ignore virtually every accepted practice of biblical interpretation. Isolated sentences divorced from a concern for over-all context prove nothing. Admittedly, it is a difficult saying, especially for those with a sentimental concept of Jesus Christ. However, what Jesus says here must be understood in the light of the gospel as a whole, as well as other aspects of the New Testament, for the general message of the totality of Scripture must guide the interpretation of specific passages.

We have already seen that neither Paul nor the author of Hebrews marks out the Jews, as a collectivity, for scorn or condemnation. In accord with Paul's Roman Epistle, John states in his prologue that the Jewish nation and people constituted Christ's "own home" and "his own people" (John 1:11). In accord with Hebrews, the relationship of Christ to the Old Testament faith is affirmed (1:17). To the woman of Samaria, in chapter 4, Jesus states that "salvation is from the Jews" (4:22). These references hardly point in the direction of Jew hatred. What, then, does Jesus mean in his statement of chapter 8?

In answering this question, we take special note of John's recurrent use of the term *the Jews*. The phrase is much in evidence throughout the gospel. Understanding the various meanings of this term will do much to illuminate Jesus' words.

It is clear that John's gospel emphasizes the distinction between the community of believers in Jesus and the followers of Judaism. Light has come into the world in Jesus Christ, and the condemnation upon men is that they choose to love darkness rather than light (3:16–19). As a religious community, the Jews were most prepared to receive the Light of the world, for they had received previous revelation of a special nature through Old Testament prophets. The Jews, then, are in a unique position. John's use of *the Jews* emphasizes, on the one hand, that Christ came to "his own people," while at the same time it expresses the tragedy and irony of their rejection. Although the term is used in various ways in the gospel, there is no evidence that John has in mind a blanket indictment of Jews as people, or as a race. Nor is it his intent to say that Jews cannot be saved, that they are all condemned, for it is obvious that most of the people to whom Jesus ministered were themselves Jews. It is therefore clear, from the total context, that the term *the Jews* has nothing to do with ethnic differentiation. Generally, the term is used primarily in connection with the religious authorities in Judaism who were opposed to Jesus. Hence, Johannine scholar Raymond Brown notes that "John is not anti-semitic."[17]

In chapter 8, Jesus presents his claims concerning himself. His words reflect the major themes found in John's gospel, that Jesus Christ is "the way, the truth, and the life." To refuse to place one's faith in Him is to walk in spiritual darkness. As many writers have observed, this claim presents a clear alternative. Either it is true or it is not. If it is not, then Christianity represents a massive deception. But if they are true, then Jesus Christ had every right to assert them, and to reject his ministry with man would constitute nothing less than opposition to God.

This theme plays an important role in chapter 8. The claims of Jesus confront the Jews' declaration that they are "sons of Abraham." The issue here pertains to identity as a child of God. Is it mere physical birth and ethnic descent? The answer of this chapter is consistent with the rest of the New Testament. It is a resounding no. The Jews contending with Jesus here are claiming a special status and spiritual protection because of physical descent from Abraham. But, Jesus challenges them on a spiritual level. "If you were Abraham's children, you would do what Abraham did" (v. 39). Abraham, of course, is a paradigm of faith, for he heard God, believed God, and obeyed God. For this reason he is among the righteous. Those who are true spiritual descendents of Abraham ought to act in the same manner. But, the people here do not. Christ has come into the world, "but now you seek to kill me, a man who has told you the truth which I heard from God; this is not what Abraham did" (v. 40).

We may understand Jesus' words in verse 44, then, as a severe warning that physical descent and blood mean absolutely nothing insofar as the great issues of spiritual reality and salvation are concerned. Human thought will be in accord with what God has revealed, or it will dwell in darkness and separation from God under the dominion of Satan. The foremost duty of a child of Abraham is to believe God. Jesus is sent from God, but the Jews who oppose Him will not believe Him even though He demonstrates through His works that He is of God (10:38). Therefore, God cannot be their father as they claim, but rather they are under the power of the devil who opposes God and Truth, who is the "father of lies."

As Raymond Brown observes, everything that Jesus says in this passage is consistent with other New Testament materials. "In his ministry Jesus reacted strongly against the claim that being children of Abraham gave an automatic status of sanctity or privilege. John the Baptist had warned that God could create a new generation of descendents for Abraham from the stones (Matt. iii 7–10). Jesus warned that strangers would come to sit with Abraham at the heavenly banquet table while the children of the kingdom would be cast out (Matt. viii 11–12)."[18]

The issues in John, chapter 8, have nothing to do with racial or ethnic matters except to condemn such designations as reasons for attributing spiritual identification with God. To interpret the radical nature of Jesus' words and the gospel's reference to "the Jews" as a text for anti-Semitism is to totally ignore this context, as well as the actual historical situation within which this encounter must be understood. Jesus' words reflect John's prologue, in which spiritual sonship to God depends not on blood or flesh, but on the reception of the One whom God has sent for the salvation of the world.

Similar charges of anti-Semitism are heard relative to Matthew, chapter 23, in which Jesus denounces the Scribes and Pharisees. Sandmel's view of this encounter is instructive in a special way, for Sandmel does not believe the passage is an authentic account of Jesus' actual words. Following the liberal Protestant views of the Bible, he regards the New Testament as being short on historical reliability in regard to its presentation of the "real" Jesus. In his view, the words attributed to Jesus are not His own, but reflect the early Church's attitudes of resentment and condemnation toward the Jews who refused to be converted to a new religion. The woes pronounced by Jesus reflect, in Sandmel's understanding, the Christian side of mutual animosities that had grown up between the early Church and the Jews. They are "partisan utterances" expressing extreme antagonisms, with the flawed attitudes of the Church attributed to Jesus, thereby enshrining this prejudice in the Christian Scriptures.[19]

This view is, naturally, convenient to "liberal" Christians who may be troubled by the alleged anti-Semitism of the New Testament. They can dismiss the entire episode as inauthentic, utilize a selective interpretation, and proceed to embrace a concept of Christ who never brought a word of judgment to anyone. This will not do, however, for Evangelicals who accept the entire New Testament as inspired by God and who recognize Jesus' statements as having the force of His own personal authority. "The conservative Christian who is determined to preserve the passage as the authentic words of Jesus needs to ponder whether he can then with intellectual honesty hold fast to a usual Christian view of Jesus as a benign and kindly soul."[20]

Two things must be said in response to this. First, there is no indication in the passage itself that all Jews are the target of the pronounced woes. Such a conclusion is negated even on the basis of Sandmel's assumption that the words are the invention of the early Church, for the early Church was clearly comprised of a good number of Jews. Secondly, the conservative Christian approaches the passage within the framework of a historic Christian theology, which understands Jesus Christ to reflect the character of the righteous God, not the "benign and kindly" soul of popular imagination. The "benign and kindly" Jesus, known through sentimental paintings that seem to find their way into every church parlor, is more a product of human tradition than of conservative theology.

Can anyone seriously hold that Jesus would never have spoken a harsh word to anyone? That He would not have spoken out forcefully against religious hypocrisy in His own time? Does the fact of Jesus' life in a Jewish context make any such statements improbable?

In fact, conservative writers and interpreters do not see this passage as a blanket indictment of all Jews. It is impossible to construe it as such under any careful manner of interpretation. What is being denounced in Matthew, chapter 23, is hypocrisy, not Jews or Judaism. Moreover, the import of this passage is often applied by the Church to itself rather than to Jews. In reality, the words of Jesus are very much in accord with those of the Hebrew prophets. If they seem harsh, what are we to think of the words of God spoken in the Hebrew Scriptures through the mouth of the prophet Malachi?

> A son honors his father, and a servant his master. If then I am a father, where is my honor? And if I am a master, where is my fear? says the Lord of hosts to you, O priests, who despise my name. . . . I have no pleasure in you, says the Lord of hosts, and I will not accept an offering from your hand. . . . Behold, I will rebuke your offspring, and spread dung upon your faces, the dung of your offering, and I will put you out of my presence. . . . For the lips of a priest should guard knowledge, and men should seek instruction from his mouth, for he is the messenger of the Lord of hosts. But you have turned aside from the way, you have caused many to stumble by your instruction; you have corrupted the covenant of Levi, says the Lord of hosts, and so I make you despised and abased before all the people, inasmuch as you have not kept my ways but have shown partiality in your instruction. (Mal. 1:6, 10; 2:3, 7–9)

Jesus' concern in Matthew, chapter 23, is the same as that expressed by former prophets. It is a concern born of the fact that God has revealed Himself and has called a people to represent the way of truth to an idolatrous world. If those in positions of leadership fail to do so, either by distorting God's revelation to accommodate their private outlook or by stressing the externals of religious observance while overlooking "the weightier matters" of true spirituality, the people who trust them continue in darkness. This is true whether in regard to ancient Pharisees or contemporary Christian theologians. In any event, it seems a crude interpretation to attribute anti-Semitism to the passage. Jesus was speaking in the tradition of the Hebrew prophets, out of concern for human salvation. If

the harshness of the indictment is the criterion for deter-
mining anti-Semitism, then one just as well might attribute
"anti-Semitism" to the Hebrew Scriptures also, which is
absurd.

We find that the Bible itself, if understood as God's
Word and revelation, does not support anti-Semitism, nor
does history reveal a connection between the adherence to
biblical authority and anti-Semitism. In periods where the
Bible was regarded authoritatively as God's Word, anti-
Semitic attitudes eased. If anyone has ever had an interest
in substantiating a base of anti-Semitism in Holy Scripture,
it would have been the Nazis, working as they were in a
nation of rich Christian tradition. But, all they could find
in the Bible was a fearsome enemy—God's righteous Word
of salvation for all, purchased by the blood of a Jewish
Savior. This is a fact that Christians must stress even today, in the face of neofascist movements that would seek
to bend the Scriptures to serve their own hate-filled purposes and anti-Semitic propaganda.

Endnotes

1. Paul L. Maier, "Who Killed Jesus," *Christianity Today* (9 April
1990): 17.

2. Dennis Prager and Joseph Telushkin, *Why the Jews?* (New
York: Simon and Schuster, 1985), 92.

3. Samuel Sandmel, *A Jewish Understanding of the New Testament*
(New York: KTAV Publishing House, 1974), 161.

4. Samuel Sandmel, *We Jews and Jesus* (New York: Oxford University Press, 1965), 146.

5. Ibid., 147.

6. Prager and Telushkin, *Why the Jews?*, 92.

7. Sandmel, *We Jews and Jesus*, 140.

8. H. H. Ben-Sasson, *A History of the Jewish People* (Cambridge,
Mass.: Harvard University Press, 1969), 646.

9. Ibid., 647.

10. Ibid.

11. Ibid., 650.

12. Ibid., 742.

13. Sandmel, *We Jews and Jesus*, 59.

14. Charlotte Klein, *Anti-Judaism in Christian Theology*, trans. Edward Quinn (Philadelphia: Fortress Press, 1975), 11–13.

15. Sandmel, *We Jews and Jesus*, 81.

16. Sandmel, *A Jewish Understanding*, 269.

17. Raymond E. Brown, *The Anchor Bible: The Gospel According to John (i-xii)* (New York: Doubleday, 1966), LXXII.

18. Ibid., 362.

19. Sandmel, *A Jewish Understanding*, 162.

20. Ibid.

∫ THREE ∫

Richard Rubenstein and "Holocaust Theology"

In the wake of the Third Reich and the Holocaust it brought, is it possible for people to believe in God anymore? The question is often asked, and when it is the God of the Bible is in view, not a generalized "life force" of romantic imagination. Indeed, the God of the Bible is implicated in the question precisely because He is a God who is said to act on behalf of His people. Where was He during the "final solution"? For many people of our century the depth and intensity of the Holocaust finally and without reservation puts the question of God to rest. Nietzsche was right—God is dead! Or, if He is not dead, He just doesn't care.

This premise is vigorously set forth by writers for whom the Holocaust is the pivotal event of modern life. One such writer is Richard Rubenstein, whose book *After Auschwitz* is still fundamental to this direction of thought. In contrast to Jewish writers like Elie Weisel, whose reflections on the Holocaust are born of actual experience as a prisoner at Auschwitz, Rubenstein's concern with the Holocaust and its implications is largely intellectual in nature.

In regard to the issue of experience, it is true that many ceased to believe in God as a result of the Holocaust or, like Weisel, came to understand God in very unsentimental terms as totally sovereign and outside all human expectation. But, it is also true that many found faith through the experience of concentration camps, as witnessed by the experience of Alexander Solzhenitsyn in regard to the Soviet *gulag*. Experience is powerful and always carries a certain authority. It does not, however, necessarily dictate true conclusions or interpretations. What makes Rubenstein's approach especially interesting is the way in which it represents an updating of the classical formulation of the problem of evil.

Rubenstein's challenging book appeared in 1966. It is a major attempt to deal with the Holocaust from a theological perspective and sets forth the author's view of the Holocaust's theological background and significance. For Rubenstein, the Holocaust is *the* theological question for modern times, an assessment with which I find myself in agreement. No theology that hopes to relate to modern life can ignore the question of God in respect to the death camps of the Third Reich. The peculiar challenge that Rubenstein sets before the Judeo-Christian faith is the assertion that the Holocaust was a disaster so vast that our images of God, humanity, and moral order have been permanently impaired.

After Auschwitz was written primarily for the Jewish religious community, but the author's questions have equal import for Christians. I can remember the silent, troubled expressions on the faces of college students listening to Rubenstein at campus appearances during the early seventies and, more recently, the incredulous, disturbed reactions to a speech by Auschwitz survivor Eva Kor. Rubenstein is right. The event raises fundamental questions as to how we understand ourselves in regard to the presence or absence of God.

Rubenstein asserts that the death camps radically challenge the Jewish and Christian recognition of a God who acts in history. After the evidences of Auschwitz, how can one believe in the traditional concept of God as sovereign, omnipotent, and caring? Inasmuch as traditional Jewish theology has interpreted major catastrophes in Jewish history as God's punishment, can one maintain this view today without also regarding Hitler and the SS as instruments of God's will? "To see any purpose in the death camps, the traditional believer is forced to regard the most demonic, antihuman explosion in all history as a meaningful expression of God's purposes. The idea is simply too obscene for me to accept."[1]

Dr. Rubenstein seems to have come to this conclusion from conversations with German pastors and theologians. Especially noted is Heinrich Grüber. These men held the conviction that the evidences of God's activity in history are primarily seen in the life and destiny of the Jewish people (a conviction shared by the majority of American Fundamentalists and Evangelicals). For Rubenstein, such a premise logically demands the conclusion that the Nazi slaughter of the Jews was God's will and "that God really wanted the Jewish people to be exterminated."[2] He claims that his objection only received "embarrassed silence" at the time of his conversations and that no "credible" answer has come forth in the ensuing years. In 1978, Rubenstein stated in *The Christian Century* that there had not yet been offered any "intellectually responsible" answer to the principle theological issue raised in his book and that the failure of the Judeo-Christian world to accept his argument witnessed to a tendency to cling to old beliefs, no matter how much evidence is shown to disconfirm them.[3]

What are these beliefs, which Rubenstein asserts have been "disconfirmed" by the Holocaust?

Not only is the existence of the personal God challenged, but the entire notion of God's activity in covenant and election. Jewish existence, as well as Christian existence, is challenged to the extent that the Jewish and Christian communities are interpreted in theological, "supernaturalist" categories. As far as the Jews are concerned, so long as they are viewed as God's chosen people, the misfortunes of history must be seen as God's will, or at least as taking place with His permission. This includes such an

event as the Holocaust. Christians are held to the same
conclusion in so far as they retain a theological understanding of the Jews as a people of supernatural vocation.
According to Rubenstein, such a view of God's decisive
activity in history leaves no choice but to interpret the
Holocaust "as God's just chastisement of a sinful Israel or
to regard that event as effectively disconfirming the theology of covenant normative to both traditions."[4]

In other words, the Holocaust forces us to conclude
either that (1) the Nazis were instruments of God's will, or
(2) the God of history, the biblical God, is false. Inasmuch
as the first alternative is repugnant, we must begin to work
out our view of life relative to the second alternative. Not
surprisingly Rubenstein's perspective leads to a death-of-
God position. The only alternative is to embrace a God
"who would not even flinch at the use of death camps to
bring about his purposes."[5]

Rubenstein likes to present this argument as if it were
invulnerable, suggesting that his interpretation can be
avoided only at the expense of one's intellectual integrity.
In truth, the argument is forceful in view of the magnitude
of the Nazi crimes and the emotional response inspired by
the Holocaust. Yet, Jews and Christians, while giving due
consideration to Rubenstein's argument, must not allow
such a profound theological issue to be decided on the
basis of emotionalism and Rubenstein's sentimental rhetoric to the effect that "a God who tolerates the suffering of
even one innocent child is either infinitely cruel or hopelessly indifferent."[6] Rather, a theological interpretation of
the Holocaust, be it Rubenstein's or Heinrich Grüber's,
must be submitted to an examination of both Scripture
and history, as well as the critical consideration of underlying philosophic premises. (Incidentally, Grüber actively
aided Jews during the Hitler period and was himself sent
to a concentration camp.)

Rubenstein suggests that the Holocaust was a unique
event, raising radically new and singular theological questions. But, is this really true? Certainly, there is nothing
unique in the spectacle of persecution, suffering, and death

in the life of a covenant community. The people of God's covenant are no strangers to peculiarly severe suffering, as the Bible itself makes clear. But, Rubenstein's argument contains the implicit premise that covenant and election necessarily guarantee a special protection from suffering in the world. Such a premise is false from a biblical point of view. Not only are the sufferings of God's people predicted and reported in Scripture, they are powerfully demonstrated in history. Did Jews and Christians during World War II suffer pain more terrible than crucified masses of Jews and Christians during ancient times? How can Rubenstein qualify the suffering of those who died in the Nazi Holocaust in such a way as to suggest that their deaths were any more "disconfirming" of biblical religion than the deaths of people crucified or eaten alive in Roman arenas? There is very little reason to see the Holocaust as any more disconfirming than the horrors of former times, unless we play a numbers game with "the six million." But, this seems crude, for as Rubenstein himself must realize, the significance of suffering is not a matter of counting heads! If the suffering of one individual child is enough to invalidate belief in a God who acts in human affairs then why should the deaths of six million people in a few years' time be any more disconfirming than the suffering of *any* individual person, past or present?

In reality, Rubenstein raises no new issue at all. Rather, he draws upon the traditional "problem of evil" as popularized by Enlightenment philosophers—i.e., if God is all-Good and all-Powerful, why is there so much suffering and evil? It is true that the Holocaust represents a unique concentration of death into a finite time span, but this has no more significance for the question of God than does the six million death-count. The problems of evil, suffering, and death are not defined by numbers of bodies or numbers of years, although this seems to lie at the root of his argument.

A closer look, then, at Rubenstein's argument reveals that although his denial of God is anchored in the Holocaust, he does not really need the Nazis to arrive at his conclusions. One suspects that his holocaust theology is more of a convenience than a necessity. The "disconfirming evidence" of which Rubenstein makes so much was around long before the Nazi death camps. The unique status of the Holocaust for the question of God and the doctrines of covenant and election is a chimera. The argument is grounded more in emotionalism than in real reflection. For this reason, it is quite possible that Jews and Christians continue to believe in the God of history in the face of Rubenstein's challenge, for the simple fact is that "the evidence" is not so uniquely "disconfirming" as he suggests. The questions raised by the Holocaust are no different than those raised by the persistence of evil in general. This is recognized by Rubenstein himself, when he writes that "the real objections against a personal or theistic God come from the irreconcilability of the claim of God's perfection with the hideous human evil tolerated by such a God."[7] This statement is candid and reveals that Rubenstein's case against God is not grounded in the Holocaust at all, although Auschwitz is for him a convenient launching pad.

Rubenstein accepts, in an apparently uncritical way, the classic formulation of the problem of evil, while ignoring the many answers to that formulation that comprise the literature of theodicy (the "justification of the ways of God"). The only alternative to a world in which human beings are free to choose between good and evil is a world in which they are *not* free to do so. If love (which is unquestionably good) is to be possible, then the world demands the kind of freedom in which beings can choose not to love. Love is meaningless apart from the potential to withhold and reject it, for love is by nature a free act. A moral world implies the possibility of immoral action. Very few people are willing to posit an amoral world of automatons as a superior proposition to one in which freedom exists. As for God's redemptive purpose in history, it is impossible for Rubenstein or anyone else to say that such a purpose is not being sustained, for one would have to be omniscient himself in order to know that.

Nevertheless, it is fashionable to blame human evil on God or to utilize the existence of evil as an excuse for denying God. But, does the magnitude of human evil radically disconfirm the biblical view of God, man, and moral order, as Rubenstein asserts? In light of the biblical evidence, it is difficult to understand this view. The Bible does not tell us that the world is perfect or free of trouble or that people of covenant are protected from tribulation. If it did, then the presence of evil would indeed be disconfirming. But, the Bible is utterly true to the human condition and does not spare the saints of God from tribulation, suffering, torture, or death. Moreover, Scripture identifies the source of evil as lying within the rebellious will of God's creatures, a source which Rubenstein seems to overlook. God is at work in history, but so is man, the fallen creature whose heart is "desperately wicked." This consideration must govern any assessment of evil and the truth of the biblical worldview. In a letter to *The Christian Century*, written in reply to Rubenstein, Abe Shapiro stated the issue precisely in recognizing that humanity "is inhuman beyond all human measure," and that the "only hope there can be is to rely on love beyond all measure—from God, through us, for all."[8] In a similar vein, Eliezer Urbach (who lost his parents at Auschwitz and a brother in a Soviet labor camp) asks if the real question vis-a-vis the Holocaust ought not to be "where was humanity when God 'has showed you O man what is good; and what does the Lord require of you but to do justice, and to love kindness, and to walk humbly with your God?' (Micah 6:8)."[9]

But, what of Rubenstein's assertion that traditional theism must understand Hitler as God's "rod of anger" against the Jews? This contention is of special concern to Christians, who see the Jewish rejection of the Messiah as inviting Divine Wrath upon disobedience. Must the Christian understand Hitler as an instrument of God?

In this matter, Rubenstein completely overlooks the significance of the Cross for Christianity and the fact that the Christian perspective is grounded in the atoning death of Jesus Christ. In Christian faith, there is the fundamental recognition that human sin has been judged already, through the person of Jesus Christ. His substitutionary death is offered on behalf of Jew and Gentile alike. From a New Testament perspective, there is no reason to assume that God would have anything to add to the suffering and death of Christ by a chastisement of the Jews collectively, or by a judgment manifested through their extermination.

The Christian is free to view Hitler within the biblical framework that identifies a hatred of the world toward God and all people identified with Him. Jew and Christian alike witness to the reality of moral law and the ultimate judgment of God. The world hates this witness. In this regard, we have the pertinent observations of Dennis Prager and Joseph Telushkin that Jew hatred in the ancient world was stimulated by the Hebrew claim that their God was, in fact, the true and only God, with the consequent implication that the pagan gods were false.[10]

Rubenstein himself acknowledges that humanity naturally rebels against any limitation of autonomy and that a world in which God is dead is one without moral restraint of any kind. Here we are in agreement. But, in this we may also see Hitler as a paradigm of the ideal of "human autonomy"—arrogantly opposed to any transcending standard of moral righteousness as expressed in the Ten Commandments or manifested in the ministry of Jesus Christ. If Hitler is to be associated with any biblical idea, the proper parallel would seem to be to the Beast of the Book of Revelation rather than Old Testament figures who brought tribulation to the Jews, such as Nebuchadnezzar. The latter retained a respect for the Jews' God and His gifts. The Beast does not, but rather exalts himself as "God." He is not an instrument of chastisement and discipline, but is a manifestation of total God-hatred and is one who "makes war on the saints." In either case, though, the biblical word places a limitation on the powers of persecution. They shall not prevail and will suffer judgment themselves while God's people shall be preserved.

History actually confirms this promise. The civilizations of Babylon and Assyria have long passed into oblivion, and Hitler's "thousand-year Reich" lasted but a few years, ending in terrible devastation. On the other hand, the Jews around the world retain much of their ancient heritage and dwell as a nation in the ancient land. And, so it will be in the future, no matter what resurrections of such God-hatreds there may be. Thousands of years of history testify to God's preservation of His covenant people and communities—Israel and the Body of Christ.

Richard Rubenstein calls upon modern man to reject historic theism. He is unclear, however, as to what shall replace it. While he dogmatizes that Judeo-Christian tradition represents an "irretrievable past," he affirms the strange notion that "omnipotent Nothingness is Lord of All Creation."[11] Judaism, for him, is the context of shared lives in an unfeeling and silent cosmos. But, what can this mean for him? His position that the universe is meaningless actually detaches him from fundamental Jewish roots, and he appears to be an example of what Prager and Telushkin call "non-Jewish Jews" who, in turning to such theological, political, and cultural radicalism actually stimulate anti-Semitic attitudes. The significance of the Jews in human history derives from their association with the God who creates, loves, redeems, and judges. It seems cruelly ironic for Richard Rubenstein to pass off this whole tradition as a literally unbelievable fraud.

His embrace of "omnipotent Nothingness" undermines his entire plea and passionate concern for the Holocaust, for if the cosmos is unfeeling and silent, with "Nothingness" as "Lord," then what difference does it make how many Jews have been slaughtered, or Christians, or blacks, or Cambodians, or whoever? Rubenstein's own conclusions—that God is dead, that humanity makes its own rules, and that there is no objective moral law by which human activity may be judged—witness to the absurdity of his own indignation, for what can it possibly rest on? It is perhaps for this reason that Jews and Christians alike have largely rejected his assessment. It has nothing to do with their inability or unwillingness to face facts. Rather, it has to do with the recognition that a philosophy so self-contradictory is absurd if not actually evil itself.

Rubenstein fails to see that the only answer to the Holocaust is the very God he denies. He is too determined to characterize God as a cosmic monster to see that without the recognition of His lordship a thousand holocausts could be perpetrated with not one thin shred of a basis for moral resistance or protest. In a subsequent book, *The Cunning of History*, he admits that in an earlier age men and women stood in awe before the reality of God's judgment. Of course, this implies a deterrent effect on evil practices. But, people no longer stand in such awe and recognition. Rubenstein laments the fact that, even if such a natural or God-ordained moral law were recognized, it wouldn't make any difference, for "there are absolutely no limits to the degradation and assault the managers and technicians of violence can inflict upon men and women who lack the power of effective resistance."[12] He assumes that there is no such law and that we must conclude that we live in a world which is functionally godless. Human rights and dignity simply depend upon the power of one's community to grant or withhold such qualities.

Traditionally, biblical theism has empowered a witness of hope in the face of the world's evil. Such is the message of the Bible. Tragically, Richard Rubenstein chooses to be defeated by Adolf Hitler and his Nazi goon-Supermen, leaving modern man with no basis for moral courage. But, Jews and Christians alike are unwilling to give Hitler that victory. The Judeo-Christian vision faces the problem of evil head-on and poses the ultimate victory of God's judgment. The Holocaust has shown us the fruit of the myth of human "autonomy." The response of humanity today must still begin, then, with a hearing of the Word of God to repent, flee from the Wrath to come, and know the riches and the mercies of God.

Endnotes

1. Richard Rubenstein, *After Auschwitz* (Indianapolis: Bobbs-Merrill, 1966), 153.

2. Ibid., 53.

3. Richard Rubenstein, "A Crisis of Disconfirmation," *The Christian Century* (30 August 1978): 798.

4. Ibid.

5. Ibid.

6. Rubenstein, *After Auschwitz*, 87.

7. Ibid., 86.

8. Abe Shapiro, "Butchered Love," *The Christian Century*, vol. XCV, no. 35 (1 November 1978): 1053.

9. Edith S. Weigand, *Out of the Fury: The Incredible Odyssey of Eliezer Urbach* (Denver: Zhera Publications, 1987), 102.

10. Dennis Prager and Joseph Telushkin, *Why the Jews?* (New York: Simon and Schuster, 1985), 83.

11. Rubenstein, *After Auschwitz*, 225.

12. Richard Rubenstein, *The Cunning of History* (New York: Harper and Row, 1975), 90.

∫ FOUR ∫

Saints in Resistance

As stated in chapter 1, there is a tendency to regard the witness of Christianity during the Hitler years to have been either nonexistent or cowardly. It is my intention here to suggest otherwise and to emphasize, not by way of excuse for the Church's shortcomings, but in the interests of understanding that the situation was unprecedented in history. The fact that Christians have learned something from the Holocaust is evident in today's context, most specifically in relation to the abortion issue. Parallels are constantly drawn with the past, and fueling Christian concern today is the hope that future generations looking back on our times will not hold the Christian faith in dishonor for failing yet again to allow its voice to be heard on behalf of those led to the slaughter.

We are constantly urged to remember the Holocaust. Memorials are appropriate, as are the other reminders. But, there is still something missing, and that is the lack of interest in and visibility for those of the Christian faith who *did* put their faith and lives on the line. In the mainstream secular literature that concerns itself with the resistance, you encounter the names of Martin Niemöller and, of course, Dietrich Bonhoeffer. Bonhoeffer is notable for his conviction that Hitler was in fact antichrist and for his part in a plot to have the Führer assassinated. A brilliant young theologian, he died by execution in the Flossenbürg concentration camp, shortly before the end of World War II.

Niemöller, leader of the Confessing Church, was also incarcerated but survived the war, and his words are frequently quoted to substantiate the claims of a failed Christian witness and to project the "guilt of Christendom" for the Holocaust.

But, certainly there is more to the story than these two men. In the interests of memory, this chapter presents capsule biographical accounts of people who did act. Compelling stories of courage and Christian integrity can be found, furnishing people today with spiritual encouragement to "stand in the evil day" (Eph. 6:11). Moreover, we need to recognize that visible Christian witness was acknowledged during the period itself. Writing in 1941, Peter Viereck, a Pulitzer Prize-winning historian and poet, called attention to the fact that "[in] Hitler's concentration camps languish not only liberals and Jews but non-political and 'Aryan' Catholic and Protestant ministers." In reference to Niemöller, Viereck noted that he was certainly the most famous voice of resistance, but surely "only one of many thousands martyred for the crime of being sincere Christians. For example, seven hundred pastors were arrested in Prussia at one fell swoop in 1935 for denouncing modern paganism from the pulpit."[1]

The following discussion is heavily indebted to Beate Ruhm von Oppen's *Religion and Resistance to Nazism*, and to *July 20, 1944*, an anthology of writings by historians concerning the German opposition to Hitler, published as a public document by the Press and Information Office of the Federal Government of Germany. Ruhm von Oppen's work is a research monograph printed in 1971 at Princeton University. It is of particular value in that it was written with the expressed purpose of addressing the criticism of the churches during the post-World War II decades. *July 20, 1944* features valuable insights and reports of the British journalist Terence Prittie, who was working in Germany during the Nazi years and whose work presents a thoughtful and fair analysis of the Church struggle and the prominent individuals involved.

Ruhm von Oppen opens the question as to whether the mainstream of criticism regarding the Church is fair and pointedly draws attention to the contemporary climate of critical opinion directed toward the Church and Christianity. "Often," she writes, "it is, I would say, an uncritically 'critical' attitude that prevails. There is something herdlike about it, and a great parroting of slogans. Much 'criticism' really falls into the category of incantation or polemics."[2]

Ruhm von Oppen wisely exhorts us to understand the peculiar conditions that existed in Germany during the Nazi period and suggests a lack of intellectual honesty in the critics of the Church for failing to have regard for the social context in which statements and actions took place, a context in which even the most innocent statement might be seen as subversive and provide reason for imprisonment or death. "There seems to be an intellectual limitation that makes it impossible for some 'critics' to read the documents they do read as they *must* be read: as communications taking place in conditions of unfreedom."[3] Ruhm von Oppen reminds us that hindsight easily serves up correct insights, and that the Church critics invariably rest their charges on the Church's failure "to utter what the critics think should have been uttered." What is more significant, though, is that even through such stringent limitations on speech and writing as were effected by the Nazis, certain communications *were* effected, despite the limitations.

> To me the lesson of the Nazi period and experience is the miracle of what, after all, turned out *not* to be completely manipulable. Resistance *was* a kind of miracle, not the thing one expected to happen. Manipulation was taken to greater lengths and backed by more horrible sanctions than ever before, I think, in the history of man. . . . The difference between the critics and the Nazis is that the Nazis found the churches in fact interfering with their manipulation,

but the critics fail to notice that interference. . . . One wonders for instance why Goebbels, the Minister of Popular Enlightenment and Propaganda, was so worried about the influence of Vatican Radio and why the police and security services were keeping such close watch over the clergy and their following.[4]

Indeed, if the churches were doing nothing other than collaborating with the regime or protecting their own institutional interests, how might we explain the statement of Count Helmuth James von Moltke in a 1943 letter to a friend in England? (Moltke was an expert in international law in an organization of the High Command, who, as an insider, worked to hold up or thwart certain Nazi policies. He was tried and executed in 1945.)

> The opposition has done two things which, I believe, will count in the long run: the mobilization of the churches and the clearing of the road to a completely decentralized Germany. The churches have done great work these times. Some of the sermons of the more prominent Bishops, Catholic as well as Protestant, have become known abroad. . . . But the most important part of the churches' work has been the continuous process by which the whole clergy, practically without exception have upheld the great principles in spite of all the intense propaganda and the pressure exerted against them. I do not know of a single parson who in a church demolished by British bombs held a sermon with an anti-British strain. And the churches are full Sunday after Sunday. The state dare not touch the churches at present.[5]

Ruhm von Oppen notes the significance of what Moltke refers to as "upholding the great principles"—the quiet, steady work of the Church in teaching and worship that did not make it into foreign news journals or historians' notebooks but which was certainly noted in the records of the Gestapo or the law courts.

Specific cases, however, make the drama of the resistance concrete and, like a modern book of martyrs, add to the "cloud of witnesses" in Christian history that may furnish us, through their examples, with requisite courage should it be called for. Following, then, are capsule reviews of the actions of a few that exemplify the course taken by many whose names will never be known except in the world to come.

Dietrich Bonhoeffer

Probably the most famous of the Protestant resisters, Bonhoeffer decided on a career in theology while still a high school student. His sensitivity to Nazi policies was probably aided by the fact that his twin sister was married to a Christian of Jewish origin. Even before Hitler assumed power in Germany, Bonhoeffer's voice was raised against fundamental aspects of his appeal. On 30 January 1933, the young theologian broadcast an attack on the Leadership Principle as it was applied in the spheres of church and state. Shortly after this, he spoke out against the mounting attacks on the Jews, declaring that the church that discriminated against members on the basis of race no longer represented the Body of Christ.[6] He was a cofounder of the Confessing Church movement with Martin Niemöller and is described as "a great teacher and preacher in it." What makes Bonhoeffer's case so interesting is that he had the opportunity to live in the safe confines of the United States where he had fled in 1939. There, some of his friends at New York's Union Theological Seminary sought to convince him that he could serve the cause of resistance far better in America. He realized, however, that if he were to have any hope of contributing to the reconstruction of his nation following the war he would have to return and face the searing decision as to "whether he wanted his own country to win and destroy civilization or the others to win and destroy his country."[7]

Bonhoeffer was part of a conspiracy to kill Hitler and was arrested in the spring of 1943 along with other conspirators. Tried and imprisoned, he was hanged on 9 April 1945. Bonhoeffer left many writings, most significantly *The Cost of Discipleship*, in which he defines his concepts of "cheap Grace" and "costly Grace" and gives definition to the biblical truth that faith without works is dead. Clearly, Bonhoeffer's life and career raises crucial moral and ethical questions. Can a Christian, in good conscience, plot the assassination of another human being, even an Adolf Hitler? Would Bonhoeffer's witness be more significant for us had he and his fellow conspirators succeeded? Or did his own death more vitally serve the Body of Christ?

Bernhard Lichtenberg

Lichtenberg was a Roman Catholic priest and dean of the Cathedral of St. Hedwig, Berlin. Prior to the Nazi rise to power, Lichtenberg had acquired a reputation for social and political activism and had been a representative of the Center party, the political arm of the Catholic church in Germany. Ruhm von Oppen writes that when the Nazis came along, Lichtenberg was already on a blacklist "and subject to police visitations and searches, but he was also suspect simply as a priest. All priests were suspect."[8] What got Lichtenberg into trouble with the authorities was prayer. (In America today, how many of us think of prayer as the radical action that it really is, and does it not astound us to know how "dangerously subversive" such an act is in certain political contexts!) Lichtenberg prayed for Jews. He prayed for them every day in his church and was supported in this effort by his congregation. He was reported to the Gestapo by a couple of women, patriotic students on a sightseeing trip to Berlin who, in 1941, had ventured into one of his services and had heard his prayers. The priest's prayers were unambiguously for the Jews, a particularly radical thing, as Ruhm von Oppen observes:

> Those girls may well have been startled to hear such a public prayer and particularly to hear the Jews *called* Jews in it. Normally it was only the enemies of the Jews who would in public call them Jews. There are on record two courageous sermons by Protestant pastors given after the nationwide Nazi-staged, anti-Jewish excesses, the pogrom of November 1938. They are documents of conscience and of bravery and led to the persecution of those who pronounced them, but neither of them used the *word* Jew.[9]

Lichtenberg had creative ways of protesting. Once, when the Gestapo had closed the Seminary of the Diocese of Berlin and confiscated its property, he took to the pulpit in a packed church and announced the Gestapo action, reporting that he had received no reply to his inquiry as to the grounds for the closing. Then, he went over to the organ and played, with maximum power, a hymn invoking the presence of the Guardian Angel with the congregation singing three verses. After his arrest, he was vigorously interrogated not only about his attitudes toward the Jews, but concerning his perceptions of Hitler based on marginal notes made in his copy of *Mein Kampf.* He told his interrogators that since *Mein Kampf* was the foundation of Nazi ideology, he was duty-bound as a Catholic priest to reject that ideology as inconsistent with Christian confession. As to the Jewish situation, they were at the time being forcibly removed from German territory, destined for concentration and death camps. Lichtenberg said, as recorded in the surviving documents of his interview:

> I am opposed to the evacuation with all its attendant features, because it is directed against the chief commandment of Christianity: "Thou shalt love thy neighbor as thyself," and I recognize my neighbor in the Jew as well, who has an immortal soul, created in the image and likeness of God. But since I can do nothing to stop this decree of the government, I was resolved to accompany deported Jews and Christians into their banishment, in order to serve them there as pastor. I want to use this opportunity to ask the Secret Police for permission to do this.[10]

In a society where even the most ordinary conversation concluded with praise to the Führer in the "Heil Hitler" exclamation, Lichtenberg forthrightly declared the principles set forth in Hitler's book to be false and contrary to Christ. "If the principles are wrong, the actions will not be right. That applies even to Adolf Hitler."

Ruhm von Oppen perceptively notes that "none of this was calculated to get him off the hook." And, it didn't, even though he was offered his release if he promised to stop preaching. After a prison term, he was sent to the Dachau concentration camp. He never arrived there, dying while in transit.

Franz Jägerstäetter

Jägerstäetter is described by Ruhm von Oppen as "a simple Austrian peasant and sexton of his village church." Nevertheless, "he was a thinking man and he thought very, very seriously about questions of religion, ethics, and politics, and their relationships." Contrary to the vast majority of Austrians who welcomed the Nazis in the plebiscite of 1938, Jägerstäetter voted against them. He had carefully observed the conflict between the Catholic church and government in Germany and had read the papal encyclical *Mit Brennender Sorge* (With Deep Anxiety), authored in German, not Latin, by Pope Pius XI, and which had fueled the fires of persecution. Although the Catholics of Austria were warmer toward the Nazis than those in Germany, Jägerstäetter knew that the conflict was fundamental. Hitler was against the Church, and the principles of his faith were at stake. When called up for active duty in the Nazi army he refused to answer the call, ignoring clergy advice to be "reasonable" and to think of the good of his family. Jägerstäetter prayed for the strengthening of the clergy, whom he charitably recognized as being made of flesh and blood that is understandably given to weakness. "This is why we should not make it harder for our spiritual leaders than it already is by levelling accusations against them. Let us pray for them, instead, that God may lighten the great tasks which still stand before them."[11]

Jägerstäetter was executed on 9 August 1943 by guillotine. His life is the subject of a biography by Gordon C. Zahn, *In Solitary Witness: The Life and Death of Franz Jägerstäetter.*

Kurt Gerstein

Active in Protestant organizations, Gerstein is notable as a man who attempted to get true information in a propaganda-ridden society in which lies were an instrument of policy. Rumors of atrocities made their way through Germany and into other countries, but how reliable were such stories? Gerstein wanted to find out, and, although "a devout Christian and an anti-Nazi," he joined the SS. Ruhm von Oppen suggests that Gerstein was motivated in this act by curiosity aroused by the death of an aunt in the Nazi euthanasia program in which older, mentally impaired, or other "non-productive" people were killed as a matter of policy. Gerstein "wanted to find out for himself what really went on." In the SS, he was assigned work in the Hygiene Department, and therefore had access to the program dedicated to the extermination of the Jews. Ruhm von Oppen writes that Gerstein, during the war, "tried to inform all kinds of people of the horrors he had seen, notably Protestant clergy and laymen, Dutch ecumenical friends . . . and a Swedish diplomat." At the war's end, Gerstein presented himself to Allied intelligence. He was perceived as a war criminal, however, inasmuch as he had been put in charge of supplies of poison gas, and there were invoices for such, signed by him. Gerstein testified that he had signed for the supplies with a view to diverting or spoiling them and that he had in fact done so with large quantities. Ruhm von Oppen writes that this claim is now generally held to be true, although at the time it was not.[12] Gertein's story is somewhat reminiscent of that of Oskar Schindler, as presented in Steven Spielberg's remarkable movie *Schindler's List*. One wonders how many more people, unknown to us, combined an outward conformity to nazism with acts that sought to undermine and subvert the movement's goals.

Gerstein was sent to a military prison in Paris, where he died by hanging in his cell. It is not known if he was murdered or died by suicide.

Bishop Hanns Lilje

Lilje was a German Evangelical, whose case shows that even the most ordinary, nonradical individual was watched and harassed, thereby letting us know that much courage was displayed even in a seemingly minor show of opposition to Nazi policies. Lilje never did resist openly, but merely tried to perform the normal duties toward his congregation (even this could be a controversial act). He believed that he should avoid open resistance in order to continue his ministry to his flock. He preached to congregations of two thousand and three thousand, and one of the most outspoken of his sermons was entitled "The Possibility of Living A Christian Life At This Present" which Terence Prittie describes as a "cautious" sermon that nevertheless brought him to the attention of the Gestapo. He suffered continual harassment and intimidation and was periodically forbidden to preach. Lilje was not a major voice of resistance and earned the scorn of critics who blame him for not doing more. Yet, even this man was interrogated for long hours and was imprisoned in Berlin narrowly escaping murder. Prittie observes: "All this could happen to an honorable and decent man, who did not set himself up against the regime. It can be imagined what happened to those who did."[13]

Heinrich Grüber

In 1936 Grüber, an Evangelical pastor, organized a "Bureau for Christians of Jewish Birth" in Berlin and was joined in this effort by a friend and fellow pastor Martin Albertz. The organization had the purpose of aiding Christianized Jews who were suffering under the Nuremberg racial laws of 1934. He also formed another association, more underground than the first, for purposes of protecting Jews and half-Jews. Both organizations maintained outreach beyond Berlin and were responsible for helping Jews emigrate prior to the outbreak of war. Passports and visas were forged on behalf of the Jews and were procured in Holland, Switzerland, and Britain. Grüber was arrested in December 1940 and sent to the concentration camp at Sachsenhausen where he suffered beatings in which most of his teeth were knocked out. He survived the war, however, and in the postwar era affirmed the Christian faith in the face of the Communist regime in East Germany. Encountering yet another round of persecution, he emigrated to the West in 1960. Upon his incarceration at Sachsenhausen, his work was carried on by Albertz, Hermann Maas, Werner Sylten, and others. These men likewise were apprehended by the Gestapo by the end of 1941.[14]

Karl Stellbrink

Stellbrink is representative of many Evangelical clergymen who refused to take the oath of allegiance to Hitler and who defied bans on their preaching. "There were many who spoke up bravely and did not hesitate to warn their flocks of the dangers of Nazism,"[15] one of whom was Karl Stellbrink, pastor of the Lübeck Lutheran Church. In Lübeck, he was close to several Catholic priests with whom he collaborated in the circulation of letters and sermons by anti-Nazi clerics like Cardinal Graf Clemens von Galen. During the allied bombing of Lübeck, on the night of 28 March 1942, Stellbrink and his Catholic friends told their congregations that they were witnessing God's judgment on all Germans for their sin in serving a tyrannical regime. Stellbrink and the priests with whom he worked were arrested in April, then tried and sentenced to death. They were executed in November. "Stellbrink is reputed to have said of his joint resistance with Roman Catholics: '*What a community we could become if we were united!* [emphasis mine]'"[16]

Paul Schneider

Schneider's story is a searing account of implacable courage and unceasing annoyance to the Nazi regime. He was dead before the war began, for, from the earliest years of Nazi rule, he was their determined foe. The year 1933 had not yet passed before he was in trouble, preaching against the Hitler Youth Organization as an attempt to deceive German youth into a non-Christian way of life. He vigorously opposed the German Christian movement and openly satirized speeches by Nazi propaganda chief Josef Goebbels. In June 1934, he was arrested for his handling of a funeral for a young member of the Hitler Youth. A

Nazi party official in attendance interrupted the service to proclaim that the dead youth had gone on to join the "Horst-Wessel Brigade" in Heaven, which drew a pointed reply from Schneider that there was no evidence that Saint Peter gave automatic entry to Heaven to members of the Hitler Youth.

In May 1937, Schneider preached a sermon based on Luke 18:31-43, a passage in which Jesus restores a blind man's sight. Schneider applied the passage to Germany, which he likened to the blind man in need of restoration. Arrested the next day, he was forbidden to go back to his congregation. After hiding out in southern Germany for some months, he returned to Dickenschied and his church in October, but was immediately arrested and imprisoned. From there he was sent on to Buchenwald concentration camp. Even there he got into constant trouble, refusing to bow the knee to Baal. His story at this point begins to read like *Foxe's Book of Martyrs*. At Buchenwald, Schneider refused to remove his hat during a prisoners' parade when the Nazi swastika flag was hoisted, an act which earned him a whipping on a rack that stretched the victim out with legs drawn up to expose the buttocks. Prittie, in his account, notes that "half a dozen lashes were usually enough to make a prisoner howl in agony. There is no record that Schneider uttered a sound."[17]

Schneider found himself in solitary confinement in a cell that often had an inch of water on the floor. Fed on bread and water, he was continually beaten by the SS overseer.

> He was tortured . . . [and] strung up by his arms, which were tied behind his back, from the bars of his cell window. His hands could be tied higher and higher behind his back, forcing his head down into a bent position. The Agony on the Cross was being re-enacted, but not as a single, awful ordeal. Schneider was strung up for hours at a time, day after day and week after week, as he fined down to a broken, bruised skeleton, clad in rags and with his body crawling with lice.[18]

Even so, Schneider would not let up on the Nazis. He would pray aloud from his cell so that other prisoners in the parade yard could hear him, calling out the name of Jesus. On occasions when the SS would shoot prisoners (sometimes just for fun), he would warn them: "I have seen this, and I will accuse you of murder before God's judgement-seat!"[19]

Paul Schneider died in July 1939, his body the victim of lethal injections (but which did not kill him) and described as "a single festering mass of cuts, scars and bruises" with legs "swollen to elephantine proportions by starvation, and his wrists were colored blue, green and red, in huge blotches. He was beaten on his deathbed by the flower of Hitler's Aryan youth."[20]

Prittie, in writing of Schneider, regards him as exemplary of the efforts of various individual churchmen who showed their loathing of nazism and who are today unsung heroes and martyrs.

Michael Faulhaber

Sixty-four years old when Hitler came to power, Faulhaber was the cardinal archbishop of Bavaria and was the first high-ranking Catholic prelate to take an unequivocally firm stand against the Nazis. A man with a particular love for the Old Testament, he stood out against the Hitler Youth characterization of the Hebrew Scriptures as "the Jew history book full of lies." He preached that no race should hate another race and that Christ, who happened "not to have been a German," was the foundation of Christianity. Immediately, then, it could be seen that Faulhaber was not going to cave in to Völkish notions of race superiority or anti-Semitism. From 1933 onward, Faulhaber had his sermons printed, with many copies made available in various churches for anyone who wanted one. Other copies were nailed to church doors. Terence Prittie was in Germany at the time, and he writes "I can remember the little crowds that gathered to read them in the late 1930s, their members standing silent and absorbed but casting the occasional surreptitious glance around them."[21]

By 1935, Germany was awash in an overtly expressed paganism, with revivals of pagan cults dedicated to Teutonic gods and attempts by the German press and media to smear the reputations of priests as sexual perverts or robbers enriching themselves through the offerings of the Church. Faulhaber took on the publication *Stürmer*, which Prittie describes as "largely blasphemous and entirely pornographic,"—a publication instrumental in starting up trials of Catholic priests for alleged immorality and/or treason. The priest's home was attacked in 1938, the windows smashed by a mob that also sought, though unsuccessfully, to set it on fire. As late as 1942, Faulhaber was preaching to his Munich congregation that Germany had been waging a war against Christianity and the Church. His primary concern was for the Church and its institutional prerogatives, and, as such, he may not seem as radical as some. However, the message that there is a sphere of life that transcends the power of the state is itself radical in a totalitarian society and dangerous to utter.

Clemens Count von Galen

Of the Catholic resisters, Galen is in Prittie's view "by far the most outstanding."[22] Ruhm von Oppen takes note of the cleric's immense prestige, pointing out that the Nazis "did not dare touch Galen during the war because they felt they would have to write off the entire population of Westphalia if they did."[23] By disposition, Galen was a patriotic German, and, at first, he did not launch open attacks on the Nazis. He was also opposed to Church interference in the political affairs of the state. He seemed "safe" so far as the party was concerned. Yet, by 1934, he was of some concern to the Gestapo as a result of sermons preached on the brotherhood of all mankind, as well as the theme of slavery to dictatorship. He also became increasingly troublesome as overt forms of pressure against the Church mounted through 1935 and 1936. An interesting occurrence took place in Galen's diocese of Münster on 4 November 1936. Nazi authorities had ordered the removal of crucifixes from schools, calling them symbols of "superstition." Galen ordered nine days of prayer, which stimulated church attendance to overflowing crowds. When a Nazi official scheduled a speech to a mass-meeting in the Cathedral Square in Münster, more than four thousand gathered and shouted him down. The ordinance against the crosses in schools was cancelled.

By the early forties, Galen was an outspoken critic of the regime, and, in 1941, he delivered a series of sermons in which he narrowed the focus to specific Nazi policies, even attacking the Gestapo. He called his flock to readiness to sacrifice all for the sake of Christian truth in stirring words of exhortation: "It may happen that obedience to God, and loyalty to conscience, can cost you or me life, freedom or home. But it is better to die than to sin." Nicknamed the "Lion of Münster," he attacked the Nazi euthanasia program and the systematic murdering of the mentally retarded and mentally ill.

> For several months we have heard reports that, on orders from Berlin, patients who have been ill for a long time and who appear to be incurable are forcibly removed from homes and clinics. As a rule their families, after a short time, are told that the patient has died, and that the body has been cremated and that the ashes can be claimed. Generally one suspects, and this suspicion borders on certainty, that these numerous cases of unexpected death among the mentally deranged are not natural, but often deliberately caused and are the result of the doctrine that it is justified to suppress "life which is unworthy of being lived." According to this doctrine, it is justifiable to kill innocent men when it is thought that their lives are no longer useful for our people and for our country. This horrible doctrine seeks to justify the murder of innocent men and gives legal sanction to the forcible killing of invalids, of the maimed, the incurable, and the enfeebled.[24]

His sermon goes on to note a letter of protest concerning the policy, an action that outraged the authorities.

What was particularly infuriating was the wide distribution of Galen's sermon through copies sent to other parts of Germany. Possession and subsequent distribution by less notable and popular priests cost a good number of them their lives.

The euthanasia program was inhibited by Galen's sermon, but continued throughout the period of the Third Reich. Nevertheless, Galen's sermons offered significant inspiration to other protest movements, notably that of German medical students in the "White Rose" movement.

Prittie records a legend about Galen. It may be based on fact, and perhaps not. At any rate, it communicates something true about this human being who was so utterly impressive as a man of God, apparently both to his friends and enemies alike. He writes:

> There is a legend that the Gestapo did, early in 1942, call on Galen, in order to take him from his Bishop's Palace for interrogation. According to the legend, Galen asked them to wait downstairs for a moment. He went to his room and dressed himself in full bishop's regalia, returned downstairs and told the waiting Gestapo that he was ready to accompany them. They decided to leave him in peace.[25]

Clearly, Bishop Galen was a man prepared for martyrdom, although to that end he was not called.

The Ten Boom Family

The story of this courageous Dutch Christian family is told in Corrie Ten Boom's autobiographical book *The Hiding Place*. The store building that housed the family's timepiece business still stands and bears the Ten Boom name in Haarlem. The family carried on a ministry to fleeing Jews during the Nazi occupation of Holland, and, upon the discovery of their activity by the Nazis, they were sent to concentration camps. Corrie lost her family to the Nazi epoch, and her story is one of great Christian love, compassion, and forgiveness. A fine feature film based on the book was produced by World-Wide films, a division of the Billy Graham Evangelistic Association, which was reviewed and praised in *Time* magazine for its quality and production values. Corrie Ten Boom's book, and the film, are good resources for the Christian community in respect to the nature and rationale of Christian witness during the Third Reich period.

Hans and Sophie Scholl and the White Rose

This brother and sister led a student resistance group in Munich in 1942, distributing clandestine writings denouncing the war and the Nazi regime. Their story is the basis of a fine German film, *The White Rose*. Hans and Sophie seem to have been led toward faith in Christ through their struggle, as their letters reveal an increasing dependency upon God as their martyrdom in 1943 approached. By the time of their activism, they were surely motivated by a growing consciousness of the reality of Jesus Christ, an awareness nurtured by their intellectual and artistic interests and encounters with various French and German Catholic authors. Hans Scholl had been inspired by Bishop Clemens Von Galen, responding that "at last somebody has had the courage to speak out."[26] Of special importance to the Scholls was the Munich professor Carl Muth, a Catholic philosopher who fostered a circle of opponents of the Nazi regime through political and theological discussion. Inge Jens writes that it was under Muth's influence that their "religious perceptions . . . acquired greater intensity and firmer definition," and that "the Christian Gospel became the criterion of their thoughts and actions."[27] On 18 November 1942, three months before her trial and execution, Sophie wrote to a friend words that express the kind of faith that must have been felt by the biblical prophets themselves:

> The only remedy for a barren heart is prayer, however poor and inadequate. . . . I'm still so remote from God that I don't even sense his presence when I pray. Sometimes when I utter God's name, in fact, I feel like sinking into a void. It isn't a frightening or dizzy-making sensation, it's nothing at all—and that's far more terrible. But prayer is the only remedy for it, and however many devils scurry around inside me, I

shall cling to the rope God has thrown me in Jesus
Christ, even if my numb hands can no longer feel it.[28]

Hans and Sophie were beheaded, at ages twenty-five
and twenty-one respectively, on 22 February 1943. Today
in Munich one may visit Geschwister-Scholl Platz near the
University of Munich, a space dedicated to "brother and
sister Scholl."

There are countless others, but the above profiles give
the picture of Christian integrity. If many Christians failed,
and if the churches as institutions failed, so be it. We must
recognize that tragedy. At the same time, we must not
allow that failure to define the story for us. Jesus said that
the gates of Hell itself would not prevail against His Church.
We dishonor those who stood in their Christian integrity
if we adopt a chic acceptance of nothing but Christian
guilt, which is so eagerly assumed by some in our day. We
also may insult the Holy Spirit of God. Do we really think
that the Spirit that creates, sustains, and binds together
the Church was asleep during the period of the Third
Reich? There is evidence to the contrary that must gain
our attention. According to many estimates, approximately
five thousand members of the German clergy were sent to
concentration camps and more than two thousand of them
died while there. It was a time, as Beate Ruhm von Oppen
notes, that called for more than just a "sense of ethics."
What was needed was a real faith in God.

> What those times required, and ours do too, was and
> is a combination of responsiveness and resistance. What
> my observation at the time and of the time led me to
> is the conclusion that the combination required a kind
> of piety and presupposed or developed religious faith.
> I have always been struck by the disproportionately
> high incidence of piety among those who did resist
> the Nazis. One had not much known or noticed such
> people before. But now, when resistance was what
> one looked for, often in vain, it was such people that
> seemed to have it and to offer it. And there were
> those, too, who under that deadly challenge devel-
> oped into such people. It was an experiential discov-

ery of religion, if you like; or, putting it another way, one might say that the man or the woman willing to undergo risks was granted faith.[29]

Endnotes

1. Peter Viereck, *Meta-Politics: The Roots of the Nazi Mind*, rev. ed. (New York: Capricorn Books, 1965), 290.

2. Beate Ruhm von Oppen, *Religion and Resistance to Nazism* (Research Monograph No. 35, Center of International Studies, Princeton University, 1971), 64.

3. Ibid., 65.

4. Ibid., 64–68.

5. Ibid., 21.

6. E.H. Robertson, *Dietrich Bonhoeffer* (Richmond, Virginia: John Knox Press, 1966), 7.

7. Ibid., 9.

8. Ruhm von Oppen, *Religion and Resistance to Nazism*, 40.

9. Ibid., 41.

10. Ibid., 45.

11. Ibid., 52.

12. Ibid., 34.

13. Terence Prittie, "The Protestant Conscience," in *July 20, 1944: Germans Against Hitler*, ed. Hans-Adolf Jacobsen (Weisbaden: Wiesbadener Graphische Betriebe GmbH, Public Document, 1969), 123.

14. Ibid., 123–24.

15. Ibid., 24.

16. Ibid., 124.

17. Ibid., 130.

18. Ibid.

19. Ibid., 131.

20. Ibid.

21. Ibid., 83.

22. Ibid., 89.

23. Ruhm von Oppen, *Religion and Resistance to Nazism*, 30.

24. Ibid., 29.

25. Jacobsen, *July 20, 1944*, 95.

26. Robert Jay Lifton, *The Nazi Doctors: Medical Killing and the Psychology of Genocide* (New York: Basic Books, 1986), 41.

27. Inge Jens, ed., *At the Heart of the White Rose*, trans. J. Maxwell Brownjohn (New York: Harper and Row, 1987), 161.

28. Ibid., 257.

29. Ruhm von Oppen, *Religion and Resistance to Nazism*, 69.

∫ FIVE ∫

Images and Their Worship

The history of art, which falls into the spectrum of my teaching responsibilities, is in large measure the history of religion. With the notable exception of the Hebrew tradition, ancient religions were intimately connected to the making of images. The power of the created image resided in its capacity to give some concrete, coherent form to beliefs and hopes. The radical and unprecedented character of the faith that the Hebrews were called to is indicated early on in God's commandments to Moses and the nation at Sinai: "You shall not make for yourself a graven image, or any likeness of anything that is in heaven above, or that is in the earth beneath, or that is in the water under the earth; you shall not bow down to them or serve them" (Exod. 20:4-5).

The issue here is not that of thwarting human creativity in the arts. It is noteworthy that one of the first people we read of in Scripture who is filled with the Spirit of God is an artist, Bezalel, also mentioned in Exodus. He is filled with the Spirit and "with ability and intelligence, with knowledge and all craftsmanship, to devise artistic designs" (Exod. 31:3-4). Such designs were to beautify the Tabernacle raised to the worship of God. What the commandment does reveal, however, is the seductive power of artis-

tic imagery to deceive, especially when the artistic enterprise is thought to reveal divine powers and to embody
them. Inevitably, this leads to a distortion that has human
beings bowing down to and worshipping the works of
their own hands and the products of their own imaginations. Hence the apostle Paul, writing to the church at
Rome, reflects on man's penchant for idolatry:

> Ever since the creation of the world his invisible
> nature, namely, his eternal power and deity, has
> been clearly perceived in the things that have been
> made. So they are without excuse; for although
> they knew God they did not honor him as God or
> give thanks to him, but they became futile in their
> thinking and their senseless minds were darkened.
> Claiming to be wise they became fools, and ex-
> changed the glory of the immortal God for images
> resembling mortal man or birds or animals or rep-
> tiles. (Rom. 1:20–2)

The issue of images is a powerful one in Scripture.
Isaiah, in a wonderful passage that exposes the foolishness
of idolatry, ridicules those who make idols as involving
themselves in hopeless contradiction, although they are
too blind to see it (Isa. 44:9–20). In the New Testament,
Paul explicitly declares to a group of Athenians, in the
greatest artistic and cultural center of the ancient world,
that God is not "like gold, or silver, or stone, a representation by the art and imagination of man" (Acts 17:29). In
saying this, he made a direct challenge to their entire
worldview and cultural tradition. Daniel and his three
Hebrew friends saw the issue clearly during the Babylonian
Captivity when King Nebuchnezzar erected a statue of
himself and required that all the people worship it. Of
course they refused, thereby inviting the wrath of the king
and the fiery furnace. Then, there is the intriguing reference to "the Beast" in Revelation, chapter 13, wherein a
great power arises, and, working "great signs," it works
deception in the human race "bidding them to *make an*

image for the beast which was wounded by the sword and yet lived; and it was allowed to give breath to the *image of the beast* so that the *image of the beast* should even speak, and to cause those who would *not worship the image of the beast* to be slain [emphasis mine]" (Rev. 13:13-5).

Throughout history, images have been thought to embody power, hence there is much human interest and fascination with them. Human art is able to accomplish impressive results, especially where the representation of nature and the human form is concerned. Although his works look primitive and untutored to our more sophisticated eyes today, one notes with interest the excitement created by the fresco paintings of the fourteenth century Italian painter Giotto. Although his drawing skills were limited (as judged by subsequent developments) and his placement of figures suggests no more than a shallow stage effect, his works were perceived to be "almost alive" by the people of the time, for by comparison with normal standards of art, Giotto's images presented a heightened sense of reality and emotional power. In a later time, during the sixteenth century, the pope himself is said to have fallen on his knees in agony imploring God to forgive him of his sins, upon seeing Michelangelo's immense painting of the Last Judgement in the Sistine Chapel. Today, the images that move us are themselves in motion—film, video, television. And, they likewise carry great power for good or evil. Two of the most memorable experiences with images that I can recall happened in movie theaters. I was a teen-ager in both cases. The first occurred relative to a film about the end of the world called *When World's Collide*. As the story progressed and the earth increasingly was assured of total destruction, I actually experienced panic and fled from the theater. The truths conveyed in the film—the vulnerability of the human condition, the certainty of death, and the implicit, though secularized themes of final judgment and "the coming end" took hold of me. Another occasion, different but no less powerful, was a response to the film *The Robe*. This was the first

Cinemascope film and was very grand in its production and sound. It was done in the early fifties at a time when historical films with a positive Christian import could still be seen. I vividly recall my emotion, which I did not understand at the time, when the character of Marcellus, played by a young Richard Burton, realizes that he is forgiven for his role in the death of Christ and pledges his life to the Lord's service. The scene presents a climax in the story, and I was haunted by this to the point that I returned to the theater on subsequent occasions just to see that one scene again.

Art has power and a certain glory. The temptation, however, is to give it more than its due and to forget that beauty itself can serve demonic as well as godly ends. This brings me to the subject of Hitler, the Nazis, and their absolutely ingenious pursuit of image-making in the interests of inspiration, the cultivation of hope, the celebration of community—positive values all—but which proved ultimately to be deception of the most destructive kind. In the Third Reich, as in any totalitarian state, all artistic media had to be brought into conformity with the vision-defining authority of its leaders. The Nazis energetically employed the arts to mold people's outlook and attitudes to embrace the National Socialist worldview. For Hitler, art served a "noble mission" as the expression "of an ideological and religious experience" as well as political will. Art served the purpose of purifying public life through absolute control of painting, sculpture, cinema, theater, press, education, and broadcasting.[1]

I have a colleague who was growing up in Germany during the Nazi years. She attended Sunday school in one of the Confessing churches. She said to me once, remembering those years: "Those Nazis! They really knew how to put on a show!" Indeed, I can recall the strange responses I experienced when, in 1950, I viewed for the first time films of Nazi rallies. I was impressed, but disturbed in a way that I still cannot articulate by the pomp, the marches, the uniforms, the flags, the orchestrated "glory" of it all.

And, this was a response from seeing a film on a small twelve inch black-and-white television screen. Not even stereo sound! What must it have been like to have actually been there in the situation. One of the more uncomfortable and humbling thoughts I have had about all this is the suspicion that if I had been there, with nothing much to guide me other than aesthetic responses, I might have been an enthusiastic participant. The mind and heart are terribly vulnerable.

Images, supported by ceremony and ritual, take on extraordinary power to the extent that they express a mythos, or story. In Christianity, for example, the impressive grandeur of Byzantine images of Christ as *pantocrator* (ruler of all) look down on the congregations in such churches from golden domes and possess power to the extent that the people can relate them to the salvation story. The Image of Christ in the dome triggers the associations of Incarnation, Life, Death, Resurrection, and Exaltation, as well as the Judgment. An entire worldview is conveyed, without which the image is meaningless. I experience this all the time in teaching. Christian art is interesting and meaningful to Christian students who know the stories and who have at least a fundamental grasp of biblical theology. Secular students, who have no context for understanding the image, often are bored and can't grasp what it is all about.

What I am saying here is that it was not enough for the Nazis to stage impressive spectacles or design flags and standards or distribute pictures of Adolf Hitler (who was not, interestingly enough, very impressive to look at anyway). No, in order for the imagery of nazism to work, it needed to serve a story and an understanding of why things are as they are and the ongoing meaning of it all. And, of course, the ideas had to be big, grand, and cosmic in scale.

That nazism was a spiritual movement is seen in the components of its mythos. We may note some of the more important features of this meaning system as follows:

1. *A Disturbed Life Situation That Needs To Be Made Right.* This element is comparable to the traditional biblical doctrine of the Fall. In nazism, the condition was the humiliation of Germany following World War I through the conditions of the Treaty of Versailles.

2. *An Enemy or Betrayer.* In nazism, the Jews functioned collectively as a kind of Satan and were charged with betraying Germany to her enemies. They were also defined in terms of disease, threatening the health of the Aryan race and German civilization.

3. *A Salvation Mission of an Individual and People.* The wrong condition is righted by a savior and those who collectively belong to him. This involves necessarily themes of struggle, death, resurrection, and glorification.

Keeping the above in mind, it is easy to see why nazism is best understood as a religion that sought its own peculiar aesthetic expressions. Some of these expressions are terribly mediocre products of artists with limited imagination and stylistic powers. Still, they are interesting for what they are meant to convey. One such example is a painting by Hermann Otto Hoyer showing Adolf Hitler in the early years of his career speaking to a gathering of his followers. The "congregation" listens intently to Hitler who stands on a box at the right of the picture, one hand on his hip, the other raised in exhortation after the manner of a preacher. The title of this painting is *In the Beginning Was the Word*, a title lifted out of the opening of the Gospel of John. Another painting of the Nazi period shows Hitler in profile, holding a swastika flag and dressed in medieval knights' armor, thus arousing the image of Hitler as a crusader.

Of more interest are Nazi posters advertising the SS and army. One such work shows a young, strong, "pure" looking man gazing resolutely into the far distance. The image is drawn as from below so that we seem to look up at the figure, giving it a heroic quality. There are also posters for the Hitler Youth showing healthy, smiling young German kids making charitable appeals, much like our own March of Dimes. Good works! A notable movie poster from the period has an image of the "archetypical Jew" showing a snarling, lecherous mouth, narrowed eyes, and yes, *horns* protruding from the forehead.

Without question, however, the paramount imaging capacity of the Third Reich was displayed at the annual Nazi party rallies held in Nuremburg. These events were spectacular and lavish symbolizations of the Nazi worldview involving an integration of visual, auditory, and musical arts in what might be properly understood as a pagan "cathedral event." Over a million people came into the city for these rallies, and Hitler would speak in sports stadiums packed to overflowing. Historians have noted the devotional fervor of these meetings, stirred up by powerful musical accompaniment and monumental architecture. Hitler addressed the assembled masses from the top of an enormous wall, appearing as a lone charismatic hero surrounded by thousands of banners and standards. At the Nuremberg night rally the "hour of dedication" was marked by a stunning pyramid of searchlights that created a luminous canopy of light over the figure of Germany's Satanic messiah. "In the darkness, surrounded by the masses of his followers, the high priest received the adulation of his people."[2]

In all of this, there was a human attempt to recreate in an idolatrous context the great scenes of worship unfolded in the pages of the Book of Revelation. The foolishness of it all is revealed by Albert Speer, Hitler's architect and the designer of the rallies. In his memoir, *Inside the Third Reich*, Speer recalls that the idea of a night rally was stimulated by party unease over the appearance of the middle and minor party functionaries. Soldiers, laborers, and SA members would look good. They were "in shape" physically. But, how to make the rank-and-file party members look impressive and disciplined? As Speer notes, "It proved a rather difficult task to present [them] in a favorable fashion. For the most part they had converted their small prebends into sizable paunches; they simply could

not be expected to line up in orderly ranks." Their appearance, in fact, had caused sarcastic remarks from Hitler.
Speer had a brainstorm: "Let's have them march up in
darkness."³ So a concern for beer-bellied party workers led
to one of the most impressive ritual occasions of life in the
Third Reich! (I wonder what Isaiah would do with that
one.)

But, the occasion would be wondrous. Speer envisioned
the grand procession of thousands of flags in the evening,
lit up by spotlights which would also cast reflected light on
the eagles crowning each flag standard. "That alone would
have a dramatic effect. But even this did not seem suffi-
cient to me." Recalling the sight of aircraft searchlights
beaming into the night sky, Speer requested and received
130 such lights for his drama. His description conveys the
sense of mystery and "holiness" resulting from the technique:

> The actual effect far surpassed anything I had imag-
> ined. The hundred and thirty sharply defined beams,
> placed around the field at intervals of forty feet,
> were visible to a height of twenty to twenty-five
> thousand feet, after which they merged into a gen-
> eral glow. The feeling was of a vast room, with the
> beams serving as mighty pillars of infinitely high
> outer walls. Now and then a cloud moved through
> this wreath of lights, bringing an element of surre-
> alistic surprise to the mirage. I imagine this "cathe-
> dral of light" was the first luminescent architecture
> of this type, and for me it remains not only my
> most beautiful architectural concept but, after its
> fashion, the only one which has survived the pas-
> sage of time.⁴

Foreign visitors witnessing these displays described
them as having a staggering sense of solemnity and beauty,
likening the effect to being in a cathedral. Even black-and-
white photography today still conveys the unique splendor
of Speer's environment of "worship."

Of course, Speer was utilizing the spiritual force that lies implicit in the interplay of light and dark. Light is a fundamental symbol of Truth, Holiness, and Hope. In the Book of Genesis, God's initial act in creation is to penetrate the darkness with Light, and in the Gospel of John the drama of Christ's coming is initially set forth in terms of "light shining in the darkness." Historically, Christian architectural tradition made much use of light through interior walls that reflected light off brilliant mosaics or, as in Gothic architecture, through stained glass. People could not help but make religious associations with Speer's setting and with the central character featured in that setting—the Führer himself.

There is no greater documentation of the spirituality of nazism than a remarkable film produced in connection with the Nuremberg rally of 1934. The film is *Triumph of the Will*, produced on the order of Hitler and directed by the German actress and filmmaker Leni Riefenstahl. It is a modern cinematic "image of authority," which uses film to accomplish what former ages utilized stone sculpture or painting to do—make an individual ruler larger than life, expressive of the superhuman and the godlike. Even today, with all the advances in film technology in the years since, Riefenstahl's black-and-white movie evokes a strange and unsettling power, a kind of macabre sense of inspiration.

Leni Riefenstahl was an interesting and remarkable woman and artist. She was not a member of the party and her appointment to produce this film brought annoyed reaction from Hitler's close associates in the party. However, she demanded and received full artistic freedom in the making of *Triumph of the Will* as well as other films, such as *Olympia*, done for the 1936 "Nazi Olympics." Speer, in his memoirs, recounts that her opponents in the party were won over after they saw the products that emerged from her work over the years.

Triumph of the Will opens with an illuminated Nazi eagle standing atop a wreathed swastika. The swastika is an ancient occult symbol, and, in sanskrit, the word carries the meaning of well-being. It is also a solar symbol. In nazism, the swastika became a *mandala*. A mandala is a symbolic form used in Eastern mysticism that expresses the oneness of all reality. It is a representation of the universe, or a consecrated area serving as a receptacle for the gods and a collection point of universal forces. Circular in form, the design elements in a mandala flow toward and emanate from the center. The Nazi swastika/mandala assumed two different compositions. Armbands and flags displayed the "floating" swastika in which the arms are tipped up diagonally while floating free of the circular border enclosing it. The effect is mysterious, active, expressing a spinning or rotating effect. Flag standards, on the other hand, displayed the "anchored" swastika in which the arms are vertical and horizontal within the circle, touching the enclosing edges. This effect is forceful, expressing an immovable, unshakable power and the evocation of an emotional sense of strength and wholeness through a combination of boldly intersecting right-angled forms and the circle, historically a symbol of completeness and eternity. The red field surrounding the black swastika in a white circle communicated strength through the design's simplicity, as well as passion and the implication of blood purity. The film's opening announces a dramatic event taking place in the context of monumental events of history:

> On September 5, 1934 . . . 20 years after the outbreak of the World War . . . 16 years after Germany's crucifixion . . . 19 months after the beginning of the German Renaissance . . . Adolf Hitler flew to Nuremberg. . . . to review the columns of his faithful followers.[5]

The historical context is presented in terms of death and resurrection and employs the familiar Christian association of "crucifixion." Also, the reality of faith is implied. This is no mere political event, but a spiritual moment of historical, indeed cosmic significance.

This theme is extended in the remarkable scene that follows. The filming is done from inside an airplane flying high above a cloud cover. Descending, we find ourselves among glorious, light-rimmed cumulus clouds, the whole sequence accompanied by gentle music expressing a quality of serenity and yearning. The political and spiritual implications are that Adolf Hitler and his movement are "born from above" and incarnate the very spirit of the universe. It is worth noting that in the context of the thirties, when rail travel was normative, there was something singularly dramatic in a leader flying to a meeting. There can be little doubt that Hitler was well aware of the symbolic advantages of flying to Nuremberg, and Riefenstahl took full advantage of its imaging powers.

As the plane descends into the cloud cover, the music communicates a playful sense of mystery and the city of Nuremberg appears below. Our initial sighting is of church steeples, then a sweeping panorama of the sharply pitched roofs of the city. Looking straight down on the streets, we are able to see the regular columns of thousands of SS troops marching as the music picks up the melody of the Nazi hymn, the "Horst Wessel Song." All is anticipation as the scene shifts to take up the point of view of those who await their Führer. We see the plane (not a very impressive one from today's point of view) descending with the music rising in power. City streets are seen again from above, with the shadow of the plane touching the marchers, then the throngs of citizens, smiling, shouting, arms raised in greeting. The music is now more martial, more intense, as the plane lands on an open field. The camera comes in close as the plane wheels around to approach the crowd. Then, with music rising with the cries and shouts of the crowd, the door opens and Hitler emerges to wild ecstasy. "God" has come to his people, descending from the skies!

This is perhaps the most impressive sequence in the entire film. Shown to a theater filled with German "believers" it surely must have been a moving and "faith enhancing" event. Other aspects of the cinematic image are compelling as well. Hitler is filmed in a car that sweeps through the Nuremberg streets, with much attention paid to the joyous expressions of onlookers. The impression is one of a nation of happy and hopeful people. As Hitler emerges from the automobile at his destination, he is filmed in a brief profile, framed in a glowing light like a halo. This image has its antecedents in the history of imperial and religious art. Roman emperors were depicted in profile on coins, and the halo and aura were used in Christian art to express the divinity of personages depicted in mosaics, frescos, and stained glass designs. Other traditional devices of exaltation are used in the film, such as showing the leader from below so as to enhance a sense of stature and size.

Flags are everywhere in this film. Literally thousands of them are carried by marching SS and SA men, while others decorate buildings and podiums. In one scene, which follows a sequence of a nighttime torch rally, a swastika flag floats gently in the morning breeze and the light of day dawns, to the sound of church bells and sweet, calming music.

The first of the mass gatherings depicted is that of workers. They march in disciplined file, carrying not guns but shovels. Nevertheless, they cry out the conviction that they are soldiers too, concluding in unison. "Here we stand, we are ready! On with Germany to a New Era!" They call out their place of origin, citing various German towns and cities, but the idea communicated is that they are one body transcending all individuality. During this part of the film, there is a remarkable ceremony in which flags, to the accompaniment of mournful, solemn music, are lowered stage by stage to the ground but then spring up suddenly. This symbolizes the theme of death and resurrection, the resurrection of the nation and German culture under the Führer. The workmen cry out, "You are not dead, but live in Germany!"

The speeches in the film given by Hitler and various other party officials reflect a confident and hopeful view of existence. There is a citing of economic regeneration and visions of people back to work. Equality is another theme that is struck. Hitler stresses the goal of a "classless society" in which people will be "peace loving but courageous as well." (It doesn't take much to detect the clever use of euphemism here. "Courageous" clearly means "aggressive," and actually negates the force of "peace.") Biblical sounding language is used at times, as when Hitler tells the masses of Hitler Youth that they "are flesh of our flesh, blood of our blood." He also plays on Christ's warning concerning the unforgiveable sin when, in reference to his SA organization he states: "He who sins against the spirit of the SA will not be affected, but whoever sins against the SA itself will be affected." Sin, then, is redefined in National Socialist usage to mean "offense to the party and its enforcers." Other themes are that of racial purity and Hitler's person as "supreme judge."

The most famous individual scene in the film is the great stadium gathering in which Hitler pays homage to Germany's war dead from World War I and addresses the SS and SA. Thousands are organized into great blocks that fill the stadium ground. Through the central aisle, walking quietly and resolutely, move Hitler and two others. They stand briefly before a large wreath that encloses a burning altar. Then, they retire. After a dazzling parade of swastika flags, brilliantly filmed by Riefenstahl, Hitler mounts a large elevated stone podium to speak. He is introduced by an SA man who declares, "We await only your command."

There follows a long sequence of SS troops marching through the city streets, moving powerfully to heroic, Wagnerian music and goose-stepping in a hard, violent harmony. Riefenstahl managed to spiritualize this display as well, catching shots of troops marching through rays of sunlight so as to almost dissolve their figures. They seem to march into the light, with its inevitable spiritual associations, be enveloped by it, then emerge from it. It is a disturbing, blasphemous image interpreting the divine call to "walk in the light." When Hitler is viewed, he is filmed from beneath, symbolically elevating him.

The final scene is set in the Krongresshalle, a long, deep meeting hall given to impressive ceremonial marches. Swastika after swastika moves past the eye of the viewer. When Hitler speaks he begins quietly, in a controlled fashion, then builds toward his customary oratorical fury. He tells the gathered worshippers that the party rally has not been merely a political occasion. Rather, it has meaning as "a spiritual meeting." He reflects that there was a time, before the party victory, when it was not easy to be a Nazi and that many of the "old fighters" were there, those who had persevered through struggle. What they wanted, he says, was "a true ideology" and to be "the *one and only power* in Germany." The total image of the party, Hitler affirms, will be like "a Holy Order" with "unchanging doctrine and organization like steel but with a flexible strategy." He concludes:

> It is our wish that this state should endure for thousands of years. . . . We are happy to know that the future belongs to us completely. . . . The idea of our movement is the philosophy of our people and a symbol of eternity. Long live National Socialism! Long live Germany!

He is then followed by Rudolf Hess, who shouts with terrifying power: "The Party is Hitler! Hitler is Germany! Just as Germany is Hitler!"

The film concludes with a solemn hymn, the "Horst Wessel Song" sung by male voices, with a final setting of a swastika flag transparentizing over silhouetted marchers filmed from below, walking against a glowing sky.

It is ludicrous, or so we think, that people would have been deceived by all of this. Yet, the power of the lie is great, and the light of spiritual discernment in the nation had dimmed. Did Hitler and his men actually believe the substance of all this symbolism? In fact, did Leni

Riefenstahl? There are some aspects of the film that would indicate that Riefenstahl knew it was all a sham. Not every view of Hitler is heroic or exalted. Close-ups catch fleeting looks of apprehension on his face, or boyish pleasure at a crowd response. There is also an ever-so momentary view of Hitler, emerging from the plane at the beginning, that seems to communicate his devious nature. It is in the face. Glancing out the sides of his eyes, he seems to be a man aware of putting on a "show" but hardly convinced of the truth of it all. These are my own personal impressions and are stimulated by scenes that, in historical retrospect, may be more given to such interpretation than would have been generated at the time.

But, we know from Speer's memoir that the people closest to Hitler referred to him in private conversation as "the Chief" and did not unfailingly go through the routine of hand salutes followed by "Heil, Hitler!" Also, he gives us a picture of Hitler as a man who was haunted by a sense of his own vulnerability, especially worried about his health and not at all sure of his place in history. Once, after a long conversation with Cardinal Faulhaber, Hitler sat quietly looking out a window with Speer as his only company and reflected on the possibility that should he fail in his mission "I shall be condemned, despised, and damned."[6] Not exactly the words of a "god" or Supreme Judge. We can only wish we had access to the substance of Faulhaber's conversation.

Does image-making lead necessarily to deceit? It would be a mistake to make that assumption, for images can serve truth as well as deception. What we can learn from the Nazi years, indeed *must* learn, is the extraordinary power that an image can have to strip human beings of elementary processes of reason and discernment. After the Holocaust, who can doubt the biblical truth concerning the human condition—that humanity is a radically "fallen" project that will seek meaning in even the most ludicrous of claims? While admiring her courage and spirit, there is much reason to doubt the statement of Anne

Frank that people are "good" at heart. The Third Reich was a vast enterprise established consciously on the premise that human beings are prone to believe a lie—if the lie is forceful and big enough. Nothing Hitler did assumed otherwise, nor can historians and philosophers easily prove him wrong. If the human race should have learned anything from the Holocaust, it is the depth of human vulnerability to deception. As the century closes, can a much celebrated modern humanity—so free, so amplified with new knowledge, so liberated from "superstition"—really look about and say that any lessons have been learned?

I write this even as human hopes have risen in the wake of the crumbling of the Berlin Wall. Yet, the memory of other, more recent holocausts is fresh and immediate, as well as the persistence of personality cults of local and national varieties. Nor is it unusual to see images of the swastika on magazine covers and in political cartoons addressing the cultural parallels between our own day and the society out of which Hitler and the Nazis arose. These images give expression to an unease, that the unholy spirit that swept the world into a firestorm of conflict is still with us and rising. One thing is certain, however, in the great energies now working to give voice to human aspiration. That certainty is nothing less than the promise of Jesus Christ that no power of darkness will destroy the Word that will endure forever. Today, as ever, the foundational role of Christian faith is that of a nourishing presence to human hopes by way of calling attention to the One True Image who reveals the Light which truly illuminates and rescues. This recognition must become part of our understanding, not only of the Holocaust itself, but of the post-Holocaust world that now, with strange admixtures of fear, anticipation, hope, and dread, approaches a new millennium.

Endnotes

1. Peter Adam, *Art of the Third Reich* (New York: Harry N. Abrams, Inc., 1992), 9–10.

2. John S. Conway, *The Nazi Persecution of the Churches, 1933–45* (New York: Basic Books, 1968), 144–45.

3. Albert Speer, *Inside the Third Reich* (New York: Harry N. Abrams, Inc., 1992), 9–10.

4. Ibid., 59.

5. Leni Riefenstahl, *Triumph des Willens* (Triumph of the Will), Chicago: International Historic Films, 1981. All other quotes from this film are from the English subtitles as presented in this version.

6. Speer, *Inside the Third Reich*, 101.

∫ Six ∫

The Occult Connections

Hitler's characterization of national socialism as a spiritual movement has received comparatively little attention in the vast literature on the Holocaust. But, why not take him seriously about his own movement? Although Hitler declared that those who thought national socialism to be solely a political-economic phenomenon knew nothing about it, political economy seems to dominate the perspectives of those who write on the subject. Even a Christian analysis of the Holocaust, such as David Rausch's *A Legacy of Hatred*, stays well within the boundaries of commonly held assumptions—i.e., the politics of racial and religious prejudice. But, George Stein was certainly correct when, in 1968, he stated that "many of the old assumptions, established presuppositions, and conventional categories of explanation cannot help us to understand Adolf Hitler and National Socialism."[1] Similarly, Carlo Ginzberg, in reviewing George Dumézil's 1939 book *Mythes et Dieux Germains*, reflects on the narrow perspectives of historiography in pursuing an understanding of the Third Reich. He notes the inadequacy of "a historiography orientated only to short-run contemporary political events" when confronted with powerful, ideologically driven movements. He writes that "in an age of rampant ideologies, precious assistance in understanding the world can come

from historians of religion and comparative mythology."[2]
In this vein as well is the shared perspective of two French
scholars, Michel Bertrand and Jean Angelini, who note
that the limitations of understanding regarding "the enigma
of our times" result from the application of "conventional
outlooks and methodologies to [the] examination of an
unconventional phenomenon."[3]

But, if German national socialism was in essence a
spiritual movement, what were the sources of its spirituality? We have already seen that the movement was supported by a heretical form of Christianity as expressed in
the German Christian church and that "the German ideology" sprang from the soil of German romanticism. Yet,
what can explain the mysterious grip of Hitler's personality on individuals around him as well as on the masses or
the peculiar mystique that nazism communicated and
continues to communicate today? Even people who have
an intellectual grasp of the character and dimensions of
evil manifested in nazism may still find themselves strangely
fascinated with old films of the Nazi era and the standards,
parades, and music to the point of feeling something akin
to inspiration.

I can admit to such, beginning in my post-World War
II childhood. This movement contained within itself a
"drawing power" of a strange and dangerous sort. In the
deepest sense, nazism constitutes a mystery, and it is precisely this quality that leads into considerations of the
spiritual, supernatural, and occultic dimensions of the phenomenon, matters that are generally overlooked by the
more notable, mainstream histories of the period. But,
any Christian perspective that avoids such matters constitutes a capitulation to secular standards alone as setting
the agenda and fails to ask what may be the most important set of questions, questions that we have the capacity,
justification, and responsibility to ask from the standpoint
of a Christian worldview.

To what degree was nazism an expression of spiritual
values residing in centuries-old traditions of occultism?
One must search out this topic in relatively obscure books,
such as Jean-Michel Angebert's *The Occult and the Third*

Reich: The Mystical Origins of Nazism and the Search for the Holy Grail, or an underground classic such as Louis Pauwel's and Jacques Bergier's *The Morning of the Magicians*. Another very unusual and fascinating book is Trevor Ravenscroft's *The Spear of Destiny*. These books will lead the reader from World War II back through the Middle Ages, the Knights Templar, and even, as in Ravenscroft, all the way back to the Cross of Christ and the Roman soldier Longinus who, tradition says, pierced the side of Jesus with his spear! But, such are the strange and surprising turns into which one is led in probing the demonic mysteries of Hitler and his Reich.

These sources of study are, it must be stated, problematic for scholars for a number of reasons. First, the assumptions harbored by the authors include the possibility of supernatural activity and are therefore automatically filed away as fanciful or sensationalist by academic researchers. Approaching history with spiritual presuppositions firmly in place, allowing them to play a role in the interpretation, appears irresponsible to historiography that is rooted in modern rationalism. Beyond this, however, the books do not always conform to accepted canons of academic presentation. Pauwels and Bergier, for example, will carry the reader along from page to page without ever giving a clearly footnoted reference. Ravenscroft's story is largely a recollection of things told to him by Dr. Walter Stein, who, he tells us, gathered historical material through a technique of research that itself involved the use of occult faculties and the practice of mind expansion. His narrative is presented with the vividness and detail of a novel, but a critical reader will be frustrated in any attempt to follow up the author's sources of information.

Yet, the connections between the Nazi worldview and occult philosophies and organizations is a matter of historical record, regardless of one's presuppositions about the supernatural, as has been demonstrated by the trenchant documentary study of Nicholas Goodrick-Clarke in his book *The Occult Roots of Nazism*. Whereas Clarke objects to the supernaturalist implications inherent in the above-mentioned works, he nevertheless demonstrates at a sociological level the influences of the occultism of late nineteenth and early twentieth century Europe upon the Third Reich leaders. As an example of "mainstream" scholarship on this subject, his work is unsurpassed. It is also worth noting here that the connections between occultism and the Third Reich may be emerging as a frontier of concern, as witnessed by a recent PBS documentary, "The Occult History of the Third Reich."

The questions pursued in these works are necessitated not only by Hitler's own assessment as to what his movement was about, but by the very nature of the phenomenon of the Third Reich itself and the sense we get from it that it represents a radically aberrant civilization resembling nothing else in our experience. Then, of course, there is the central presence of the occult symbolism of the swastika as a binding image and rallying icon.

Although Hitler, on the evidence of Hermann Rauschning's memoirs, was impressed with the nature of occult societies and manifested evidences of a madness resembling demon possession, the depth of the Nazi attachment to occult knowledge and tradition is not widely recognized. Mainstream history and intellectual life do not see such matters as having fundamental importance to an understanding of why the world takes the shape that it does. Passing references are made to Heinrich Himmler's "mystical streak," and William L. Shirer notes Houston Stewart Chamberlain's demon-driven inspiration,[4] but it remains unthinkable that occult mysticism provides a fundamental key to understanding the Order of the SS or the character and behavior of Adolf Hitler. So it is that Alan Bullock admits that Himmler had "faith in the stars" while describing Hitler as a "rationalist and a materialist" in matters of religion.[5] That assessment, while comfortable to modern academic naturalism, is difficult to accept in the face of the Nazi phenomenon itself. The "heretical" historians mount a contrary argument that the Nazi leaders seem to have possessed a deep and abiding interest in occult matters, including initiatory rituals and their implicit powers, secret doctrines concerning world history and the development of various peoples and races, and

the quest to rediscover and possess ancient forms of esoteric "knowledge" (gnosis) known to a long-since vanished
civilization of great power and racial superiority. Indeed,
it is the thesis of one such writer that Adolf Hitler was no
mere dabbler in occultism, but that the Führer was a full-
fledged magician of staggering power.[6]

History knows of a "primordial tradition," constituted
of a secret knowledge of the powers of nature and matters
of human origins. Traditionally, this gnosis was known
only to an elite of persons who, through rigorous spiritual
preparation and purification, were initiated into a knowledge of such vast and important mysteries. The "initiates"
were people who possessed not only secrets of natural
powers but who may have been able to exercise hidden
capabilities of human consciousness as well, or what occult
researcher Colin Wilson has identified as "faculty X." This
occult tradition affirms the existence of powers that tran-
scend the normal, natural limitations that seem to impose
themselves upon the mass of humankind. This is knowledge thought to be absolute, ultimate, and revelatory of
the essential meaning of reality itself. According to the
occult mythos such powers resided in a great civilization
of ancient times that fell into destruction through corruption and decadence. Through the centuries, however, there
have been certain men of "higher consciousness" who have
preserved the memory of these mysteries and passed them
on to a select group of initiates through secret societies
and initiatory cults. The legendary "search for the Holy
Grail" and the medieval alchemists' search for "the
Philosopher's Stone" are related to this gnostic tradition
of a secret transformative power of life. According to the
heretical historians, such occult knowledge and power was
the precise quest of Hitler and other Third Reich leaders,
a quest suggested in such events as Heinrich Himmler's
formation of an institute of occult research, the Ahnenerbe,
and his dispatching of explorers to Tibet to find traces of
ancient Nordic mysteries.[7] The Nazi search for occult power
has shown up as a theme in American popular culture,
too, in such films as the Indiana Jones adventure *Raiders
of the Lost Ark*.

What was the mythical, ancient origin of these psychic and spiritual powers? What were the civilizations of old, alleged to be populated by a superior race of beings, and what connections do such matters have with nazism?

Some answers are suggested by the participation of key Nazi leaders in a mysterious "Thule Society," existent in the Germany of the 1920s and 1930s. Mainstream historians look at the society as a cover organization for political activity, which it surely was. Yet, considerably more is suggested by the fact that Thule was the capitol city of a mythical civilization of Hyperborea, which according to occult tradition flourished in the ancient world long before the historic civilizations of Egypt and Greece. Vestiges of the Hyperborean civilization were to be found in the more well-known mythical civilization of Atlantis spoken of by Plato. Although standard history does not acknowledge the existence of these civilizations, the occult tradition affirms their historicity within the context of its own worldview. The significance of the Hyperborean myth for nazism is suggested by the fact that Alfred Rosenberg, Adolf Hitler, and other Nazi leaders were initiates in the society that bears the name of the Hyperborean capitol, Thule.

The Hyperborean myth is a version of the universal human notion of a great civilization of antiquity that established a primordial "golden age" of life on earth. Possessing an incredible power resulting from their knowledge of the secrets of nature, the Hyperboreans were physically beautiful to an incredible, godlike degree, and the myths suggest some elements of extraterrestrial intelligences. According to Jean-Michel Angebert, it was on such legends that the Germanic peoples based their pagan religion and occult political aspirations in the twentieth century. Furthermore, the myths were powerfully communicated through such literary and theatrical works as Goethe's *Faust, The Ballad of the King of Thule* and Richard Wagner's *Parsifal.*

These myths tell of a lost power, a lost grandeur of immense significance—a loss related to the Fall of Man and periodic catastrophes that mark turning points between the end of one age and the beginnings of another. Of importance in this connection is the occult history of mankind as found in the writings of Helena Blavatsky, a woman related to a family of Russian nobility and whose mystical doctrines provided the foundations of the theosophical movement. The significance of these ideas for important elements in national socialism are grossly underestimated, if not ignored by conventional history. According to the researchers of *The Occult History of the Third Reich*, there is a direct link between such occultic "knowledge" and Hitler's elite military organization, the SS.[8]

How was this so? The answer lies in a string of social and philosophic associations and movements that had significant currency in the Germany of the early twentieth century. Among the more educated and aristocratic elements of German society there was a kind of nostalgia and yearning for a glorious past that had vanished. The technological and urban elements of modern life threatened to wipe away even the memory of a former time characterized by simplicity in human relationships and a harmony between man and nature. During the thirty-year period from 1880 to 1910, German society experienced a flourishing of interest in the occult, largely influenced by the "Theosophy" of Helena Blavatsky. By the time of World War I, a significant occult subculture had developed in Germany and new groups devoted to occultism were arising in Vienna. Various spiritual cults flourished among the disciples of the *lebensreform* movement, which emphasized nature, physical health, and spirituality as a way of reforming German life and restoring at least some measure of purity to the human condition. Vegetarianism, physical exercise, earth-worship, and a search for occult knowledge provided such movements with their fundamental orientation, and, to quote Peter Viereck, it would be left to the later Nazi "romantic incantation and mass ecstasy" to "reawaken the elemental powers of pre-civilization days."[9] Stirring the interest among such people were the doctrines of Madame Blavatsky, especially those concerning race.

Occult "science" provided an alternative to normal materialistic science, which was understood to neglect spiritual realities and the emotional life. The occult worldview stressed humanity's relationship with the cosmos as being rooted in correspondences between the microcosm (the part) and macrocosm (the whole). "These new 'metaphysical' sciences gave individuals a holistic view of themselves and the world in which they lived. This view conferred both a sense of participation in a total meaningful order and, through divination, a means of planning one's affairs in accordance with this order."[10]

Blavatsky claimed that in 1888 she had travelled to Tibet, where she was initiated into the gnosis of the "Great White Brotherhood," a secret and hidden elect of "adepts" who command knowledge of the ancient mysteries of life and destiny, as well as occult powers of communication such as telepathy. Although declining to claim that she herself was an adept, Blavatsky nevertheless affirmed that she was in telepathic communication with the "masters" and that it was they who revealed to her the occult history of the human race.

According to this "history," the world went through various cycles, or ages, and within each age there were to be found various "root races" and subordinate "sub-races" that spring from them. Blavatsky identified an "Astral Race," which was pure spirit and the highest form of existence. In her system of thought as expressed in *The Secret Doctrine*, racial evolution proceeds in a pattern of descent from superior spiritual life forms to the less spiritual, more material forms, but then ascends again. The first human stock was projected by higher and semidivine beings out of their own essences. The present day humanity that we know is the fifth root race in the fourth evolutionary "round" and was corrupted by the incarnation of astral entities into matter and the intermixing of spiritual races with beasts. The Atlanteans were the fourth root race, the last of the divine races, and were the authors of civilization as we know it. The Aryans of the present fifth root race are their descendents. Interestingly, Semites (Jews as well as Arabs) are cited as "later Aryans" but degenerate in "spirituality" while being perfected in "materiality." In Blavatsky's "Theosophy," the various races have varying degrees of spirituality. Some are destined for greater advancement toward spirituality through subsequent incarnations, while others will be swept aside into oblivion by the changing conditions of the evolutionary cycles.[11]

Eventually, German occultists came to assert that it was in the German peoples, more so than in any other, that Aryan blood could be found. Their thought constituted a development known as "Ariosophy," defined as "occult wisdom concerning the Aryans."[12] Two very influential voices in this movement were Guido von List and Jörg Lanz Von Liebenfels.

In his popular writings, List formed a synthesis of the Völkish ideology, occultism, and theosophy. He claimed that the ancient Teutons had practiced a religious understanding emphasizing human initiation into the mysteries of nature. This "Wotanism," as it was known, "stressed the mystical union of man with the universe as well as his magical powers"[13] and sought to understand the present in terms of a remote, imaginary past that "legitimized a variety of social, political, and cultural ideals such as racism, magic, and hierophantic élitism."[14] List asserted an ancient order of priest/kings, an *armanenschaft*, allegedly responsible for all government and education in ancient society, a position held by virtue of the priests' superior wisdom. He claimed that this ancient order, along with its gnosis, had been preserved secretly through the centuries of the Middle Ages by such groups as the Knights Templar and the Rosicrucians and that it continued to exist in modern times awaiting an opportunity to establish a glorious Aryan realm in Europe. List's plans for society called for "ruthless subjection of non-Aryans to Aryan masters in a highly structured hierarchical state. The qualifications for education or positions in public service, the professions and commerce rested solely on their racial purity."[15] It is interesting to note that List favored the year 1932 as the year in which such a state would be initiated. His ideas became popular in the German military, and many soldiers joined the German Order, a secret society governed by a council of twelve initiates. The nature of this order was to influence the later Nazi SS organization, whose officers met in a council of twelve in a renovated Westphalian castle in imitation of King Arthur and his Round Table. The SS, under Heinrich Himmler's direction, also engaged in archaeological explorations to seek evidences of ancient Aryan civilization and thereby demonstrate modern German continuity with the ancient ancestors.[16]

It was only as these racial myths fused with Darwinian notions of evolutionism that the real danger and evil of the Nazi racism could find an ideological soil in which to take root. In England, the new science of "eugenics" was being fostered—a process through which human society could breed itself into maximum "fitness" against the onslaught of overbreeding "lower" racial types. As the idea spread to Germany, it came to be known as "racial hygiene" and in turn found ready acceptance among the German occultist groups. Gradually, the occult doctrines of race blended with the eugenics movement to form an atmosphere in which "the fit" were to be bred into maximum purity while the lower, non-Ayran races would be weeded out and become extinct.

"Racial hygiene" was popularized by Georg Lanz, also known by the more aristocratic name of Georg Lanz Von Liebenfels. In his journal *Ostara*, specific prescriptions for racial purification were set forth in the interests of actually breeding the "Superman" into existence.[17] For the "lower races," Lanz advocated deportation, enslavement, incineration, or their use as beasts of burden. Nicholas Goodrick-Clark observes that "both the psychopathology of the Nazi holocaust and the subjugation of non-Aryans in the East were presaged by Lanz's grim speculations," as well as Heinrich Himmler's *lebensborn* maternity organization, which developed baby factories utilizing brood-mothers in eugenic convents, serviced by pure-blooded Aryan SS males given the privilege of polygamy.[18]

In 1907, Lanz founded the Order of the New Temple, an organization inspired by the medieval crusader order of the Knights Templar. Through his publication and secret fraternal order, Lanz sought to develop a religious worldview blending the occult doctrines of race with eugenics. What he called "Theozoology" was an occult religion of race that assigned the decline of the Aryan race to the practice of bestiality, through which Aryan humans had interbred with subhuman species, thereby giving birth to mixed races whose very existence threatened the rightful position of the Aryan.[19] For Lanz, the Knights Templar were the knights of the Holy Grail. But, what was the Grail? Not, as in popular imagination, an object such as the cup used by Christ during the Last Supper, but rather a gnosis holding the key to racial purity. He believed that the Grail was an electrical force representing the psychic powers of the Aryans and that the Crusades of the Middle Ages had really been an attempt to hold back "inferior" races from the East. The ultimate goal of Lanz was to harmonize art, science, and ethics in an occult religion dedicated to the purification of the Aryan race in all nations. "Lanz wanted to stir the gods lying dormant in man, to endow him once more with the divine strength which would restore to him his original power."[20]

Adolf Hitler was a regular reader and avid collector of the journal *Ostara*. The goals outlined by Guido von List and Georg Lanz were ultimately served by the various Nazi programs of mass death, concentration camps, and the formation of the SS as an initiatory cult of racial purity from which would be bred the pure Aryan Superman. The SS would be the racial elite of the New Order, formed after the concern of the Führer who had posed the question to Hermann Rauschning: "How can we arrest racial decay? Shall we form simply a select company of the truly initiated? An Order, the brotherhood of Templars around the holy grail of pure blood?"[21] By 1934, the SS, under the leadership of Heinrich Himmler, was well on its way to becoming a mystical, initiatory order dedicated to bringing forth the restored Aryan purity.[22] Fueled by the racialist mysticism of German romanticism and occultic myths, SS members would be able to execute with dreadful and implacable severity the strategies of the "final solution," for these men operated on the premise that not all that merely appeared to be human was, in fact, human. SS documents sought to convince the order's members that "the sub-human, this apparently equal creation of nature, when seen from the biological viewpoint, with hands, feet and a sort of brain, with eyes and a mouth, nevertheless is quite a different, a dreadful creature," a mere "imitation of man with man-resembling features, but inferior to any animal as regards intellect and soul. . . . For not everything is alike that has a human face."[23]

The Nazi racist myth, then, had roots deep within an occult gnosis that envisioned a lost humanity of racial purity and power. Added to this influence was the mysterious drawing power of symbols of ancient origin including the prime Nazi symbol, the swastika.

The power of symbols is lost on many Christians today. I have heard even a fundamental symbolic act like baptism referred to as "just" a symbol, and that from Baptists! Nevertheless, the significance of symbols was not lost on Hitler. He knew well that symbols could touch the deep yearnings of the human mind and heart. After all, he had been an aspiring artist. Some would maintain that he remained an artist, albeit a demonically motivated one, throughout his political career. The symbol, Hitler knew, was a form through which ideas and values could be communicated. Yet, beyond this capacity was an element of transformative magic that underlies the purposes of virtually every initiatory cult in the world. Masonic authors of our own day, for example, stress the significance of initiation as the power of symbolic communication to affect the psyche of the initiate.

Although much information on this matter is lost due to the violent destruction of the Third Reich, it is possible to trace certain fundamental connections between Nazi symbolism and occult tradition. Angebert notes that the very colors of the Nazi party (black, white, and red) have origins in the ancient Persian gnosis of Manichaeanism, in which the same colors were used in priestly vestments. Such a corollary points "to a continuity of a diffuse esoteric element whose historical significance has yet to be appreciated."[24]

The swastika emblems of the Third Reich, fused with this color scheme, created a symbolic environment of substantial strength and mystery. It is not likely that Hitler chose the swastika symbol in ignorance of its historical meanings which in various ways express cosmic and world energies. Some scholars think that the swastika was the form of an instrument used by the Brahmans of India for lighting the sacred fire. Others see in it the representation of life moving toward perfection and transmutation, ideas of fundamental significance for an ideology promulgating myths of racial perfection and the Superman. Helena Blavatsky had much to say about the swastika, and her definition is not at all at variance with the implications of the symbol as employed by national socialism. She wrote of it as the "hammer of creation," a referent to the "invisible Kosmos of Forces," a sign that is "at one and the same time an Alchemical, Cosmological, Anthropological, and Magical sign" born "in the mystical conceptions of the early Aryans." It is "the Alpha and Omega of universal Creative Force."[25]

The swastika is a symbol of great antiquity, being found in all parts of the world, and it was used in various contexts in Europe prior to the Hitler years. But, with Hitler's use of it, the form took on an altogether new effect. Konrad Heiden observed that the bold, heavy bars within a circle had the effect of "an iron octopus, a monster, aggressively reaching out in all directions—hence its menacing and frightening effect." It gave Hitler, Heiden notes, "one of his mightiest magic weapons. . . . An uncanny power emanated from the mysterious sign."[26]

But, Angebert notes another important element of the Nazi swastika—its reverse orientation from the historic pattern. The arms of the Hindu swastika indicate a counterclockwise rotation (this is known as the Sinistrogyrate swastika), and in this orientation is implied the idea of mankind entering into alliance with forces of destiny, a covenant assuring protection. The reverse orientation, or Dextrogyrate swastika, carries a different meaning pertaining to the principle of destruction, the forces of man acting upon destiny and sometimes against destiny. "The swastika can then tap the maleficent forces of the universe and become a sign of catastrophe and death."[27]

Beyond the swastika, other Nazi symbols derived from ancient Runic symbols. In German tradition, such symbols, which originate in ancient times, had magical properties of divination and were thought to impart courage and wisdom, as well as to assure victory. In the thought of the Thulist Rudolf John Gorsleben, the runes were believed to be conductors of a subtle energy animating the universe and therefore had power to influence the material world and the course of history itself.[28] The "SS" is derived from a runic symbol which looks more like a double "thunderbolt." Runic symbols had double meanings, functioning on one level as vehicles of thought and language, while at the same time working as a design to impart sacred, esoteric meanings. "Runes were used in every important act of life to exert a favorable influence and to protect men from charms and evil spells. . . . In giving to the Nazi elite formations the double SS runic sign, it is quite obvious that Hitler wanted to show his attachment to Nordic esotericism."[29]

There is also an apparent connection between initiatory traditions in the occult fraternities and nazism's manner of conceptualizing the German nation itself. In all esoteric traditions, there are three stages, or degrees, of initiation and a triple-staged conceptualization of the human race. There are "pneumatics," or spiritually enlightened ones; "psychics," or those who are spiritual; and thirdly, the "hylics," whose consciousness and concerns are merely physical. Corresponding to this division within the gnostic initiations was the classification pattern of "initiates," "adepts," and "masses." In nazism, the Führer and his elite associates constituted the spiritually elevated Pneumatics, or Initiated ones. The Psychics (or Adepts) were represented by the party, while the rest of the nation constituted the Hylics. It would appear, in this interpretation, that the Third Reich was a kind of initiatory gnosticism fused with political power in the service of realizing esoteric myths pertaining to the recovery of lost human powers—powers lost through racial decay.

In the underground classic *The Morning of the Magicians*, authors Louis Pauwels and Jacques Bergier trace these connections.[30] In England, the Order of The Golden Dawn had been founded by Samuel Mathers in 1887 as an offshoot of the English Rosicrucian Society. The society claimed a number of famous British intellectuals and writers including Arthur Machen, W.B. Yeats, and *Dracula* author Bram Stoker. The society was formed for purposes of pursuing ceremonial magic, initiatory powers, and esoteric knowledge. Mathers claimed to be in contact with "Secret Chiefs" from whom he received a higher wisdom, but whose presence he described as overwhelming and terrible. He believed these beings to be humans, but possessed with awesome and superhuman powers. He described his meetings with them as physical, concrete ones which left him in a state of near exhaustion accompanied by cold sweats, difficulty in breathing, and bleeding from the nose, mouth, and occasionally the ears. Had Mathers encountered a Being who embodied the goals of occultic magic—the development (or the recovery) of Hyperborean or Atlantean powers, an example of the "Superman"? However we may interpret this report, it is clear that Mathers' experience is familiar and not at all surprising in light of the occult tradition or even contemporary stories of our day regarding "spirit" contacts and communications. At any rate, the goal of ceremonial magic and occult meditation is precisely that of transcending normal human consciousness and ability. The crux of the matter is the release of hidden divine potentialities in man.

Such was the goal of a German society that bears some connection to the English Rosicrucian and Golden Dawn groups, the "Luminous Lodge," otherwise known as "the Vril Society." Pauwels and Bergier learned of this movement from Dr. Willy Ley, a German rocket expert who had fled Germany in 1933. The community of the Vril was founded upon ideas expressed in a novel entitled *The Coming Race*, written by the English Rosicrucian Bulwer Lytton (author of *The Last Days of Pompeii*). In this work, "he set out to emphasize the realities of the spiritual world." Considering himself to be an Initiate, Lytton expressed

the conviction that there are beings endowed with superhuman powers who "will supplant us and bring about a
formidable mutation in the elect of the human race."[31]
Such beings, he held, are psychically advanced to the point
of having acquired godlike powers. The members of the
Vril Society, according to Dr. Ley, believed that they had
access to secret knowledge that could enable them to
"change their race" so as to become the equals of such
Supermen. Transformation would come through "internal
gymnastics and concentration," or what is in our day referred to variously as "meditation," "centering," or
"psychotechnology." The Vril is identified as the enormous energy of which normal humanity uses only a
miniscule proportion but which is the nerve center of
humanity's potential divinity. Whoever masters the Vril
will attain not only self-mastery, but mastery over others
and the world as well. In the mythos of the Vril Society,
the superhuman Lords will manifest themselves, and those
who have not made alliance with them will become slaves
of a new civilization.

These notions connect up with the Thule Society, which
included in its membership Alfred Rosenberg and Adolf
Hitler. In view of their presence, a closer look at this
society is in order, for it was within its shadows that Hitler's
spiritual outlook may have been formed.

In 1923, the leader of the Thule Society (which had
the swastika as its emblem) died, leaving a prayer addressed to his friend Karl Haushofer expressing the hope
that the Thule Society would continue to exist and change
the world. His name was Dietrich Eckhardt, a German
poet, playwright, and journalist who over the previous
three years had been the constant companion of Adolf
Hitler, instructing him in the skills of writing and speaking. To Eckhardt is attributed the development of Adolf
Hitler's extraordinary, seemingly magical powers of the
spoken word, the veritable "mediumship of his oratory."[32]
Some researchers also believe that he instructed Hitler in
"the secret doctrine," although Goodrick-Clarke holds this
to be fanciful and unsupported by credible evidence.
Nevertheless, there is the strong likelihood that the mythos

of higher beings and the great knowledge possessed by the primordial Hyperborean race played a role in Nazi racism. According to the Thule legends, the Hyperborean powers had not completely vanished from the earth. This knowledge was the possession of higher beings who would reveal it to the Initiates, enabling Aryan Germany "to dominate the world again and be the cradle of the coming race of Supermen which would result from mutations of the human species."[33]

Pauwels and Bergier see here the beginnings of what they call the "magic socialism" of nazism. It was not, however, until the influence of Karl Haushofer was felt upon the society that it became "a society of Initiates in communion with the Invisible, and became the magic center of the Nazi movement."[34] Haushofer was a general in the army and a professor at the University of Munich. He had paid numerous visits to India and the Far East and is said to have been initiated into one of the more important Buddhist secret societies while in Japan. Possessing a keen interest in geopolitics, Haushofer was powerfully gripped by a Tibetan legend that told of a great society that had flourished thirty or forty centuries ago in the region of Gobi, which had subsequently been transformed into a desert as the result of some mysterious catastrophe, perhaps of an atomic nature. According to this legend, the survivors had migrated to northern Europe and also toward the Caucasus. These survivors were Aryans and representatives of the original race from which all humanity had descended. Haushofer declared the necessity of returning "to the sources" of the human race through the conquest of Eastern Europe, Turkestan, Pamir, Gobi, and Tibet. Another version of this story has it that the masters of the Gobi civilization fled to a vast underground encampment in the Himalayas where they divided into two groups—the masters of Agarthi and the masters of Shamballa. The former was a center of meditation, the latter a city of violence and power "whose forces command the elements and the masses of humanity and hasten the arrival of the human race at the 'turning-point of time.'"[35] Trevor Ravenscroft expresses the view that the

Adepts of Shamballah were understood "to foster the illusion of materialism and lead all aspects of human activity into the abyss."[36]

This strange story perhaps explains certain weird aspects of the Third Reich. For example, in 1926, a small Tibetan community had settled in Berlin, and, when the Russians entered Berlin, they found among the corpses about a thousand individuals of Himalayan origin clothed in German uniforms! According to Ravenscroft, this was a community of adepts in occult knowledge willing to support the Nazi cause. They were known in Germany as "The Society of Green Men," and Adolf Hitler met regularly with the leader of this group, an individual noted for powers of clairvoyance and capacities of prediction.[37]

The myths of the secret societies, indeed the whole occult outlook, will appear absurd and fantastic to many people, especially academic historians who find it difficult, if not impossible, to think that such ideas could have had a real, even history-making impact in the ongoing arena of human affairs. The real issue, however, is the extent to which they influenced the historical movement of national socialism. That they did so seems certain, no matter how much the connection may be ignored by conventional histories. Nazism would seem to be very much in the mainstream of the intellectual and spiritual ethos of the later nineteenth century, with its skepticism toward traditional Christian meaning structures and a rising tide of curiosity and commitment to occult "alternative altars." Hermann Rauschning made the striking observation that the political element, for Hitler, was "for him only the foreground of a revolution which he pictures on the most stupendous scale," a revolution rooted in the conviction "that man exists in some kind of magic association with the universe."[38] He also testifies that Hitler found attractive the "one dangerous element" implicit in the Masonic mysteries (most of which he thought harmless), namely the formation of a "priestly nobility" connected to esoteric doctrines imparted through the medium of symbols and mysterious rites in degrees of initiation. The party must be "an Order . . . the hierarchical Order of a secular priest-hood."[39]

The ideal of an emergent new humanity is the central idea of occult gnosis, as well as a hope born in the heart of rationalistic, materialistic modernism, as suggested by the evidences of the French Revolution and Marxist-Leninist dogma. And, in this milieu, the leader principle is urgently affirmed, calling for the appearance of someone who models and embodies the qualities of the new humanity. But, René Guénon's reflections in this regard are haunting. Writing prophetically in 1921, he identified the dangerous implications of the occultist and spiritualistic vogue throughout Europe. Various "messianic" figures had emerged to form cults of followers but had faded into the shadows as their limitations came to light. "But who knows what the future has in store?" he wrote. "When you reflect that these false Messiahs have never been anything but the more or less unconscious tools of those who conjured them up, . . . one is forced to the conclusion that these were only trials, experiments as it were, which will be renewed in various forms until success is achieved, and which in the meantime produce a somewhat disquieting effect." Might there not be, he wrote, "something far more dangerous which their leaders perhaps know nothing about, being themselves in turn the unconscious tools of a higher power?"[40]

And, might not the same be said of national socialism itself, that it constitutes a trial experiment of some sort, a smaller version of a project that will yet show itself on a worldwide scale in the future? Although it is outside the scope of this book to give detailed consideration to biblical eschatology and prophetic interpretations of the Book of Revelation, the Third Reich certainly presents itself as an expression of the great conflicts of the endtimes. Indeed, many people living at the time thought that they were seeing the literal enactment of biblical prophecy. Angebert offers the warning that

> those who induced Germany to embrace the swastika
> are not dead. They are still among us, just as they have

been in every era, and doubtless will continue to be
until the Apocalypse. National Socialism was for them
but a means, and Hitler was but an instrument. The
undertaking failed. What they are now trying to do is
to revive the myth using other means.[41]

The dream of human transformation, wrought from
the activation of inherent spiritual forces and applications
of technology remains an active "hope" today in the various dresses of the "New Consciousness" or "New Age"
movement. Is this the newest breeding ground for yet
more political expressions of antichrist? (see chapter 7).

Did Adolf Hitler himself possess supernatural powers?
Or, conversely, did supernatural powers possess him?
These, of course, are questions that lie beyond the scope
of "normal" historical inquiry. Nicholas Goodricke-Clarke,
for example, considers such speculation as taking the Nazi-
occultism connection out of the realm of the history of
ideas. Yet, the world continues to wonder at the strange
powers wielded by Hitler, powers to inspire devotion among
the masses, to mesmerize a nation. And, this from a man
of so little outward stature or charisma! To entertain the
question is not to overlook the admitted effects of the
Nazi propaganda machine under the leadership of Joseph
Goebbels. Nor is it to discount Hitler's intense practice of
gestures and facial expressions to generate dramatic effects in his oratory. Still, perhaps Angebert is onto something fundamental when he describes Hitler as a "modern
sorcerer" possessed of prophetic, mystical, and visionary
character. Always convinced of his role as a man of destiny, Hitler could fill audiences with what Konrad Heiden
described as "awe" and the sense "that a new phenomenon has entered the room" in the form of a "thundering
demon."[42] As Otto Strasser wrote of him, Hitler was "like
a sensitive membrane which records the vibrations of the
human heart" and "was able . . . to make himself the
sounding-board of our most secret desires, of instincts
often the least acknowledgeable, of the intimate sufferings
and revolts of his people."[43]

Hitler, as he is described by certain observers, had
qualities not unlike those attributed to various spiritual

and cult leaders of our day (I recall a conversation with a man who described a literal force, a discernible physical power radiating from a Yogi with whom he had come in contact in California). One of Hitler's secretaries noted his power to impose his will on people and the release from his person of "that magnetic fluid which brings us close to people or, on the contrary, alienates us from them."[44] Others have remarked about the strangeness of Hitler's eyes and his "radiance" that drew people into his own mysterious interior life. But, there was another side to Hitler's strange presence. In his memoir of conversations with Hitler, Hermann Rauschning noted the Führer's sleeplessness and restless nocturnal activity in terms of "manifest anguish" and dread. "Hitler wakes at night with convulsive shrieks. He shouts for help." An informant, whom Rauschning credits as a reliable source, described Hitler as shouting wildly about a fearful presence in his room. "He! He! He's been here!" Did he see something similar to the "secret chiefs" of the Golden Dawn encountered by Samuel Mathers? Rauschning reports these words of Hitler: "The new man is among us! He is here! . . . I will tell you a secret. I have seen the vision of the new man—fearless and formidable. I shrank from him!" Rauschning was truly puzzled and troubled by the Hitler "phenomenon," stating that "[it] is terrible to think that a madman may be ruling Germany. . . . But how comes it that so many visitors are charmed to the point of ecstasy over this man, and consider him an outstanding genius?"[45]

This bizarre account is interesting and worth noting for a couple of reasons. First, it penetrates the normal propaganda set forth in the interests of feeding the Hitler myth. But, neither does it seem out of character with what we know of Hitler. It is not too difficult to imagine this man of such awesome strangeness acting in such a manner. Neither is the described behavior inconceivable in light of the experiences of people who have been drawn into the darker regions of occultism through initiation and contact with "spirit guides." Certainly, in a day when we read of best-selling books which have been dictated by disembodied spirits, and first-person stories of "close encounters" with UFO aliens, it is a reasonable speculation that Hitler may have been so influenced. The particularly dreadful dimension of it, however, is that we are not dealing with a Charles Manson, a Jim Jones, or a David Koresh, but the leader of a powerful European nation.

However we may think of these matters, there is nothing here that should prove shocking to a Christian, biblical worldview. Christian appraisals of the Holocaust would do well to keep in the forefront Paul's haunting words to the Ephesian church: "For we are not contending against flesh and blood, but against the principalities, against the powers, against the world rulers of this present darkness, against the spiritual hosts of wickedness in the heavenly places" (Eph. 6:12).

Pauwels and Bergier make the observation that any attempt to view the Third Reich purely from the standpoint of political economy or racial prejudice is doomed to superficiality, no matter how many pages of text are generated. The Third Reich constituted the brief triumph of magic, and even the Allied powers that had defeated this decidedly "other" civilization did not adequately understand that the war had been at its root a spiritual conflict. The ghastly, shattering perversion of the Holocaust cannot be understood within the normal categories of Western morality and science, for it was wrought by those who conceived of themselves as possessing a consciousness "beyond Good and Evil." For a moment, the alternative historic tradition, heretofore submerged into a secondary position by theology, science, and doctrines of progress, came to the surface thinking to accomplish its vision. With Pauwels and Bergier we can agree: "We must beware of this idea of a mutation. It crops up again with Hitler, and is not yet extinct today."[46]

Endnotes

1. George H. Stein, ed., *Great Lives Observed: Hitler* (Englewood Cliffs, New Jersey: Prentice Hall, 1968), 173.

2. Carlo Ginzberg, *Clues, Myths, and Historical Method* (Baltimore: Johns Hopkins University Press, 1989), 134–35.

3. Jean-Michel Angebert, *The Occult and the Third Reich: The Mystical Origins of Nazism and the Search for the Holy Grail*, trans. Lewis A.M. Sumberg (New York: Macmillan Publishing Company, 1974), x. The name "Jean-Michel Angebert" is the joint signature of Michel Bertrand and Jean Angelini.

4. William L. Shirer, *The Rise and Fall of the Third Reich* (New York: Simon and Schuster, 1960), 105.

5. Alan Bullock, *Hitler: A Study in Tyranny* (New York: Harper and Row, 1962), 389.

6. See Gerald Suster, *Hitler: The Occult Messiah* (New York: St. Martin's Press, 1981).

7. H.R. Trevor-Roper, *The Last Days of Hitler* (New York: The Macmillan Company, 1947), 21.

8. *The Occult History of the Third Reich, Part II: The SS: Blood and Soil* (Batavia, Ohio: La Mancha/Castle Productions, distributed by Video Treasures, Inc., 1991).

9. Peter Viereck, *Meta-Politics: The Roots of the Nazi Mind*, rev. ed. (New York: Capricorn Books, 1965), 299.

10. Nicholas Goodrick-Clarke, *The Occult Roots of Nazism: The Ariosophists of Austria and Germany, 1890-1935* (Wellingborough, Northamptonshire: The Aquarian Press, 1985), 29.

11. Helena Blavatsky, *The Secret Doctrine*, vol. 3 (Wheaton, Illinois: Theosophical Publishing House, 1971).

12. Goodrick-Clarke, *The Occult Roots of Nazism*, 227.

13. Ibid., 50.

14. Ibid., 55.

15. Ibid., 64.

16. Richard Grunberger, *Hitler's SS* (New York: Dorset Press, 1970), 32–33.

17. Suster, *Occult Messiah*, 35.

18. Goodrick-Clarke, *The Occult Roots of Nazism*, 97.

19. Ibid., 94.

20. Angebert, *The Occult and the Third Reich*, 237.

21. Hermann Rauschning, *The Voice of Destruction* (New York: G.P. Putnam's Sons, 1940), 229.

22. *The Occult History of the Third Reich.*

23. R.J. Rummel, *Democide: Nazi Genocide and Mass Murder* (New Brunswick, New Jersey: Transaction Publishers, 1992), 80.

24. Angebert, *The Occult and the Third Reich*, 194.

25. Blavatsky, *The Secret Doctrine*, 108.

26. Konrad Heiden, *Der Fuehrer*, trans. Ralph Manheim (New York: Howard Fertig, 1968), 143–44.

27. Angebert, *The Occult and the Third Reich*, 196.

28. Goodrick-Clarke, *The Occult Roots of Nazism*, 157.

29. Angebert, *The Occult and the Third Reich*, 200.

30. Louis Pauwels and Jacques Bergier, *The Morning of the Magicians*, trans. Rollo Myers (Chelsea, Michigan: Scarborough House, 1991), 140–52. Originally published in France under the title *Le Matin des Magiciens* in 1960.

31. Ibid., 148.

32. Suster, *Occult Messiah*, 117.

33. Pauwels and Bergier, *The Morning of the Magicians*, 193.

34. Ibid.

35. Ibid., 198.

36. Trevor Ravenscroft, *The Spear of Destiny: The Occult Power Behind the Spear Which Pierced the Side of Christ* (New York: G.P. Putnam's Sons, 1973), 255.

37. Ibid., 256.

38. Rauschning, *Voice of Destruction*, 253.

39. Ibid., 240.

40. Pauwels and Bergier, *The Morning of the Magicians*, 151.

41. Angebert, *The Occult and the Third Reich*, xvi.

42. Robert G.L. Waite, *The Psychopathic God: Adolf Hitler* (New York: Basic Books, 1977), 208.

43. Angebert, *The Occult and the Third Reich*, 232.

44. Ibid.

45. Rauschning, *Voice of Destruction*, 247–57.

46. Pauwels and Bergier, *The Morning of the Magicians*, 148.

∫ Seven ∫

Our Cultural Parallels

The Nazi years indelibly mark our interpretation of life in the years since the Third Reich's destruction. We are "post-Holocaust" people. The event colors our view of human nature and history as does no other event of modern times. The amount of literature, analysis, and artistic expression generated by the events of the years 1933 through 1945 boggles the mind in terms of sheer size as well as variety of subject matter. Studies in history, economics, sociology, psychology, art, science, religion, and occultism all contribute to the corpus of Holocaust literature. The only other event stimulating such a degree of interpretation and concern is the Life, Death, and Resurrection of Jesus Christ. With a strange symmetry of Light against Darkness, Jesus and Hitler are the two individuals on the human stage about whom more has been written than any other subject.

What is it about the Third Reich that will not leave us alone, that obstinately refuses to slip away into history? Why, fifty years after the events, are passions still aroused to keep their memory alive? And, what is there about it that causes some to adopt the absurd position of denying that it ever happened at all?

The answers are not as obvious as we might initially think. The temptation is to refer immediately to the vast numbers of people killed, and leave it at that. The fact of six million Jews and some millions of other people put to death for ideological and racial reasons carries tremendous weight in itself. Yet, even genocide does not explain the peculiar hold of the Holocaust on our consciousness. Nor is it unique. Stalin's Terror Famine in Ukraine exterminated seven million people in a single year's time (1933–34), yet his action remains a little-known event in history and is remembered with relative detachment. No, the fascination we have with the Holocaust and the Third Reich that generated it is not motivated solely by a horrified reaction to the fact of genocide. There is something here that is more than history, more than a need to grasp causal relationships expressed in political and cultural analysis. That "more" is, I submit, grounded in modern humanity's self-conceit and the nervous realization that virtually every fundamental component of the "modern" worldview is shattered by the evidences of the Holocaust. The Holocaust is the final, heavy proof that the myth of a "post-Christian world" liberated from superstition and intellectual conformity is false as to its premises, promises, and realities.

As stated in chapter 1, the twentieth century began in optimism. Modern humanity would be different. With intellect fired by the vision of "progress" and fueled by a confidence wrought by scientific discovery, the utopian dreams of ages would be realized. The ascent of man would not be characterized by material improvement alone, however, but humanity would see an allied upward movement of spirit as well. Great claims were made, in the nineteenth and early twentieth centuries, concerning man's achievement in the sciences and arts as foundation stones of a man-designed, man-governed city of God. Consider, for example, the statement of James Smithson, founder of the Smithsonian Institute, engraved in the stone face of the Institute's Museum of History and Technology in Washington, D.C. "Science is the pursuit above all which impresses us with the capacity of man for intellectual and moral progress and awakens the human intellect to aspiration for a higher condition of humanity."

In a similar vein, although with a focus on the arts, the words of William Rockhill Nelson engraved in the frieze of the Nelson-Atkins Museum of Art, Kansas City, read: "Through art we realize our perfection. . . . Art still has truth—take refuge there."

These statements do not merely reflect isolated, private notions of particular individuals. They reflect a climate of opinion that was, at one time, quite prevalent among western intellectuals and artists. They are precious ideas of modern life. But, who can take them seriously in the wake of the Holocaust or, for that matter, the various other disasters of modern totalitarianism? Is it not now clear to any thinking person that human science and art lack the intrinsic virtue that is often attributed to them? Have we not seen clearly enough that these much exalted human activities can, like anything else, be brought into the service of the demonic as well as the good?

One would think that the twentieth century permanently puts to rest the notion that humanity's fulfillment would be established through a human wisdom freed of the old ideas of virtue implicit in the worldview of the Hebrew and Christian Scriptures. Dostoyevsky's reflection that if God is dead, then all things are permitted, has been proved conclusively in the history of our times.

Which leads me to offer a challenge to modern, liberated, secular, neopagan man: It has often been fashionable to indict the Church for its past—the Crusades, the wars of religion, the Inquisition, the Salem Witch Trials (and on and on whenever fault can be found). You know the saying: "Look at all the evil that has been done in the name of religion!" Religion most assuredly means Christianity in this indictment, and you utter it so as to suggest that doing away with Christian faith would free man from evil. Your new world was to free us from all that through a new man molded by the realization of secular utopian dreams. Never did you, oh new man, have greater power over nature, or more information, or communications, or freedom from "superstition" with which to build! And, where has your vision led us, but to a dark labyrinth more terrifying than any Inquisitor's chamber. You look back on your century of dominance and see the death plague of your own doing, spawned by "autonomy" from the offense of moral law. And, you look ahead with an insistent, irritating question underlying all that you can envision. "Can we survive?" Whatever the failings of the Church in history, and we can and must admit to them, you—self-authenticated "modern man"—are a joke beyond compare! It is time to stop looking at the Middle Ages and turn your critical powers to the examination of what you have wrought.

The Holocaust makes us uneasy because it puts at issue two opposing views of human nature: the modern notion of human perfectibility owing to intrinsic "goodness" and the traditional biblical revelation of man's radical "fall," which displays at the very depth of things a heart that is desperately wicked beyond understanding. Where does the actual evidence lie?

It could be argued that in spite of everything, the world has learned its lesson. Another Holocaust is impossible. Unlike the 1930s, we have something to look back on to help our understanding. We are able to recognize the danger signals. And, indeed, one would think we could make use of the past and its warnings. But, such does not seem to be the case. Everywhere in today's context we hear comparisons of one kind or another between our own time and the principles active in Germany during the Nazi years. The phrase "ethnic cleansing" is reported in our newspapers as a euphemism for extermination of despised peoples, and, in Germany itself, we see the macabre renaissance of neo-Nazi street marches, swastika flags and all. Even the language of medicine, especially in relation to such matters as abortion and euthanasia, is hauntingly similar to concepts active during the days of the Third Reich. We, too, hear our own versions of "life unworthy of life." We, too, commit living humans to our own kinds of "special handling." What do such parallels suggest for the future and destiny of our own civilization?

It is difficult to know where to begin or how to limit

such an inquiry. Myriads of issues arise to claim important space in any such discussion. However we approach it, we must recognize that more than mere politics is involved. The deeper issues are spiritual and cultural, but, most fundamentally, they have to do with a society's sense of truth. I will approach the question, then, in relation to four primary considerations that seem to me to define a core of concerns that may be applied in various specific circumstances and contexts. They lie at the center of our present vulnerability and define the increasingly Fascist "tone" of today's social reality. These concerns focus on (1) the debasement of language and its effect upon thought and spiritual life; (2) the dilution of education into propaganda and the service of ideological agendas; (3) pervasive cultural despair and fragmentation; (4) and the illusion of political solutions and utopian dreams.

Any consideration of the dynamics of tyranny will lead inevitably to the question of language. It does not escape our notice that the Bible's scene of the Fall of Man into Judgment and Death occurs in the context of a distortion of what God Himself had commanded. The Serpent initiates conversation with Eve by ignoring the context of God's allowance that the humans could eat of every tree of the garden, then proceeds to deny what God has in fact spoken. The effect on Eve is inevitable. Her powers of discernment are clouded and disaster follows. Humanity comes under the despotic power of the "god of this world."

This lesson cannot be lost on history and our examination of specific events. George Orwell, in his classics *1984* and *Animal Farm*, symbolized in the clearest manner the relationship between language distortion and human vulnerability to despotism. In their own way, these two towering novels are commentaries on Genesis. In the stories, language becomes a tool for distorting reality. Language, being the instrument of thought, is the close ally of spiritual discernment. But, without meaningful patterns of communication based in conceptual clarity, effective thought is impossible. For this reason, it is troublesome to see the way our culture treats language. We have become a society of euphemisms, with words constantly used to *obscure* meaning rather than to *reveal* it. Examples abound and are found in virtually all walks of life. Perhaps the most guilty culprits, however, are professionals in government and education, but religion is not far behind. The extent to which we are negatively affected in these areas constitutes a large measure of how vulnerable we are to massive deceit.

The practice of obscure communication in contemporary education and political life immediately recalls the atmosphere of irrationality expressed by Orwell. Charles Sykes has called attention to what he calls "profspeak," a form of discourse that enables educators to inflate even the most trivial subjects to apparent importance or to make common sense observations sound like profound, original insight through the use of obscure jargon and convoluted syntax. The clever use of language becomes a *substitute for real thought.* But, the contemporary problem of language goes beyond a mere love of jargon and pretentious word usage. Today, in such academic movements as Deconstruction, the very validity and cognitive efficacy of language itself is increasingly under attack. That such intellectual directions bear direct consequences for the human condition is clear when we recognize the root importance of concepts for the human ability to think. Ayn Rand, author of another anti-utopian story, *Anthem*, has cited the issue of concepts as "philosophy's central issue," and, in a study of epistemology, she implied a relationship between language and human vulnerability to deceiving voices. Since human knowledge is gained and maintained in conceptual form, the core concern is the validity of concepts. "Do they refer to something real, something that exists—or are they merely inventions of man's mind, arbitrary constructs or loose approximations that cannot claim to represent knowledge?" What is at stake, Rand maintains, is nothing less than "the cognitive efficacy of man's mind." Undermining the confidence we have in the conceptual level of consciousness is the key to the negation of man's mind.[1]

In every tyranny, be it local, national, or global, political or spiritual, the capacity for independent thought must be suppressed; and inasmuch as the thought process works itself out with concepts, expressed verbally, the corruption of language and the depth of its use can only aid and abet the careers of authoritarian despots who would dilute concepts into mere slogans. Language becomes a purely emotional force, the servant of images that have no necessary relation to reality. This, of course, is the essence of propaganda and the evil of it. Nobody was more perceptive of the potentials for the exercise of power residing in the distortion of language than Adolf Hitler. In *Mein Kampf*, he wrote that "the art of propaganda consists precisely in being able to awaken the imagination of the public through an appeal to their feelings," with language serving "a systematically one-sided attitude towards every problem that has to be dealt with."[2]

Thought is a process of applying abstractions—words and concepts—to reality. Indeed, the way we learn words in the first place, put them together, and the assumptions we make regarding the validity of our concepts represent processes of knowing and condition the entire atmosphere of communication. There is a direct link, then, between issues of language and concerns for social destiny. Anyone who doubts this would be well advised to go to their local video store and search the foreign films section for a movie entitled *The Wansee Conference*. This German film tells the story of how Nazi party officials determined strategies for the "final solution," a euphemistic slogan given to the project of mass extermination of European Jews. The use of language is fascinating and the script has the virtue of recreating the actual conversations of these meetings. The discussion is conducted purely in terms of cost-analysis and the language of efficiency. There are no references to *people*! There is no hint that the problem under discussion is how to kill millions of human beings while minimizing the financial costs!

Today, the very survival of our civilization and culture may turn on a rediscovery and renewal of our respect for words. Words constitute a common storehouse of symbols and, as such, make communication possible, in the same way that commonly understood symbols in visual art made the meaning of painting and sculpture accessible to everyone during past centuries. Look at the confusion in the visual arts today, brought about by the radical subjectivity of visual symbols, and then imagine the consequences when language, which is much more fundamental to our social processes, similarly breaks down.

Create a critical mass of people who cannot discern meaning and truth from nonsense, and you will have a society ready to fall to the first charismatic leader to come along. Thus, we see the dangers in such trendy intellectual movements as Deconstruction. Here we encounter a philosophy of art and literature that offers the premise that no text, no statement, has objective meaning. Deconstruction, which has settled into various elite universities across the country, operates from the standpoint of a doctrinaire skepticism about the truth-value of language. It has been characterized by the art and literary critic Roger Kimball as an approach afflicted by an "infatuation with the thought that language is always so compromised by metaphor and ulterior motives that a text never means what it appears to mean."[3]

Thinking back to the Genesis story, this technique of invalidating knowledge of the truth is revealed to be very old indeed! It incarnates itself anew, now in academic garb as literary criticism theory. Christians make a big mistake in ignoring such trends, thinking that it is all so much ivory-tower conversation. At the heart of it, as author George Steiner has emphasized, is the issue of metaphysics and considerations of theology. Once we penetrate the obscure jargon and technical pretensions of Deconstruction, we will find, according to Steiner, a repudiation of a view of reality rooted in a recognition of *logos*—the word that is truth and which communicates that which is true.

In his book *Real Presences*, Steiner points to the ultimate Word-act, this being the creation of the world by the Word of God, which, as ultimate and absolute intelligence, invests the created order with intelligibility, meaning, and truth, employing language as a vehicle of knowing. In the *logos* understanding of reality, words have truth value as avenues of knowledge and communication. "For deconstruction, however, there can be no foundation speech-act, no saying immune from un-saying. This is the crux."[4] In Deconstruction, all correspondence between world and word is denied. Jacques Derrida, a French theorist of Deconstruction, has recognized that the fundamental issues are not merely philosophical or linguistic, though, but rather theological and that it is a matter "of the meaning of meaning as it is re-insured by the postulate of the existence of God."[5] Deconstruction holds, then, as its central premise, that the Bible's claim that "in the beginning was the Word" is meaningless.

One of the more baneful impacts of this truth-denying philosophy is the notion that all ideas, works of art, literature, philosophic outlooks, are determined solely by issues of race, class, and gender. This has fueled the attempts of many academics in the United States to delegitimize the Western heritage as little more than the biased product of dead, white, European males, disparagingly cast in the acronym DWEMS. Raised to the prime status, as a consideration in judging the merits of a work, is its origin in the race, social class, or sex (and "sex orientation") of an author or artist, giving rise to a number of ominous educational trends even at elementary and secondary levels of education. Diane Ravitch's characterization of ethnocentric trends in contemporary education sounds a note disturbingly reminiscent of "blood" philosophies of the past. In an article to the membership of the Phi Beta Kappa honorary society, she notes that certain forms of "multiculturalism" are teaching children "that their identity is determined by their 'cultural genes'—that something in their blood or their racial memory or their cultural DNA defines who they are and what they may achieve."[6] Supposedly, the goal of such programs is to foster the "self-esteem" of students, rooting this result in racial pride. One textbook for such a program asserts that black people "have a physiological superiority in the areas of physical coordination and spiritual access to energy and vibrations from the environment," and that African-Americans are endowed with "special intellectual and physical talents" due to high levels of melanin.[7] Is any of this essentially different from "Aryanism"? Is the contemporary "cult of ethnicity" anything more than a composition of minifascisms whereby people seek a false basis for pride in "blood" that distinguishes them from the common humanity that we all share? The danger of it is clearly perceived by historian Arthur M. Schlesinger, Jr., who sees in such movements an intensification of resentments and antagonisms between groups and "ever deeper . . . wedges between races and nationalities."[8] But, such is the product of an increasing acceptance of a fundamental notion—that language is meaningless. Our "intellectuals" are literally pulling up, root and branch, the very basis of the communication of Truth with the consequence that no premise, no reality can be perceived to apply in any unified or unifying way to our universally shared human condition. It is not mere coincidence that in the wake of this breakdown in rationality we should see the rising tide of ethnic hatreds and capricious violence.

In his 1993 book *Modern Fascism: Liquidating the Judeo-Christian Worldview*, Gene Edward Veith, Jr., unfolds the dimensions to which contemporary Deconstruction and "post-modern" ideology is rooted in old-fashioned historic fascism and asks the question: "What will the 'post-contemporary' movement look like, once the postmodernists have successfully discredited objectivity, freedom, and morality? What sort of society will be erected on the rubble, once the Western tradition is deconstructed?"[9] Sidney Hook, shortly before his death, noted the desire of such academics to use university humanities departments as staging areas for political action and made this observation:

> It was a mere fifty years ago that we were hearing about Aryan and Jewish physics and proletarian biology. Today once more there is talk of race, gender,

and class not as a subject of scientific study but as characterizing the scientific approach itself. Nonsense, the literature reader will say. To be sure—but we have learned that nonsense, if unchecked, will kill.[10]

A more direct association of Deconstructionism and Post-Modernist theory to the Holocaust has been made by Michael Howard in a review of Gertrude Himmelfarb's thought on the matter.

> We know what happens when people actually put these "value free" principles into practice; we saw it only a generation ago on a horrific scale in the Holocaust. Gertrude Himmelfarb shows how the post-modernists have reacted to the challenge of the Holocaust. Paul De Man, one of their major gurus, displayed at the time personal cowardice and later moral hypocrisy. Another, Jacques Derrida, has tried to evade the problem by emitting a dense cloud of unintelligible verbiage. Their followers merely frown portentously and say that the Holocaust itself must be "problematized"—that is, argued away.[11]

Once language is allowed to run its arbitrary course apart from reality, truth, and traditional understandings, virtually anything is possible. Such may be the most important cultural lesson to be learned from the Third Reich. Consider, for example, that in Nazi Germany countless individuals were killed in the euthanasia program under such rhetorical devices as "disinfection," and "death by natural cause" covered the practice of starving people to death. Indeed, in the justification of anti-Semitism, a key element in the genocide of the Jews was the use of the language of medical science—through which Jews were conceptualized as a "diseased race." Killing Jews was to heal an infection![12] Centers for the killing of mentally retarded and physically handicapped children were given titles like "Children's Specialty Centers" where the children could receive the "best of modern therapy"—i.e., death by injection or drug overdose![13] In reading of such matters, one cannot help but be struck by the parallels between such use of language and our own contemporary practices of

smoothing over the realities of abortion and other forms
of violence, such as assassinations or the human carnage
wrought by war. We may also wonder about the eventual
outcome of a confluence of certain trends that see religious faith defined as mental illness,[14] combined with the
politicization and nationalization of health care in a society increasingly given over to the art of euphemism.

Nor is theology, the guiding intellectual discipline of
the Christian faith, innocent from the processes that seem
to be carrying a great civilization to an abyss of chaos.
Nowadays, it is anybody's guess what certain concepts mean
in the life of the Church. Concepts like "evangelism," "salvation," "kingdom of God," or even "Christ" are likely to
mean whatever the particular individual using them desires them to mean. They are central, fundamental concepts of Christianity and, yet, have lost much of their
objectivity in the twentieth century, especially in the major
denominations of Protestantism. When the forming discipline of the Christian intellect abdicates the responsibility
for meaningful discourse in a context of objectively defined language, it undermines the very possibility of spiritual discernment.

Any consideration of the Third Reich and the Holocaust entails an understanding of what was accomplished
by the Nazis as a result of confused and distorted language, theological and otherwise. That there was so much
talk of "God" and "Christ" in the writings of Völkish
philosophers gives reason for serious reflection. The disengagement of Christian concepts from historical meanings was crucial to the deception. In today's context, we
may be struck by how little the word *Christ* actually means,
even as used by some theologians and ministers. Continuing to operate from the higher criticism's dichotomy between the "Jesus of History" and the "Christ of Faith," the
word *Christ* has become a vague notion that can mean
almost anything.

This became vividly apparent to me through a couple
of conversations with churchmen—those of the "mainline"
variety. I asked one of these men, a prominent ecumenical
pastor, who Christ is. "Is Christ God?" I asked.

"Oh, yes. Yes, of course. Christ is God," he replied. So far, so good. But, not much further. My next question went a step further. "Is Jesus Christ, the man of Nazareth, God?" Pause. Troubled facial expression. "Well, I say Christ is God."

"That's not what I asked. I asked if *Jesus* Christ is God."

"And I say that 'Christ is God.' That's it. Actually, I think we are both saying the same thing, we just have a different language system."

Indeed.

On another occasion, with another minister, I inquired as to who he thought Jesus Christ really was. The question was linked to a discussion of "social action," various expressions of which this minister lauded as examples of obedience to the call of Christ. Obedience to Christ, however, is an issue that rests on the question of His identity and character. Who is He that we should obey Him?

When I asked my question, this ordained minister of the gospel simply replied, with some discomfort over the question, that there was no point in "getting hung up over religious language." Looking back, though, we can see that if ever the German people needed to do anything in the years of the late nineteenth and early twentieth centuries, it was to clarify "religious language." The fact that they did not, that so many accepted "creative" theology and intuition over the authority of Scripture and the cloud of witnesses in the tradition, led to their shame and destruction.

Recent years have shown that almost any extreme of ideology or use of force can be justified in the name of an arbitrary "Christ." The danger was evident to Edward R. Norman, who in 1979 wrote of "the most remarkable of all the changes that have occurred within Christianity during the past 20 years," a process known to sociologists and religious historians as politicization. Norman defines this process as

> the internal transformation of the faith itself, so that it comes to be defined in terms of political values. . . . Christianity today is, in this sense, being reinterpreted as a scheme of social and political ac-

tion, dependent, it is true, upon supernatural authority for its ultimate claims to attention, but rendered in
categories that are derived from the political theories
and practices of contemporary society.[15]

Arthur C. Cochrane, responding to Norman's analysis,
wrote that "the present politicization of the Gospel bears
frightening similarities to the 'German Christian' movement which identified Christianity with the ideology of the
National Socialist revolution."[16]

Recent history affords no more direct a parallel between the Fascist church of Nazi Germany and the contemporary political gospel than was evident in Sandinista
Nicaragua, a situation boldly clarified by Humberto Belli
in his book *Breaking Faith*. Belli, a former Sandinista, writes
of the Sandinista attempt to forge a unity between the
Church and the party's guiding Marxist ideology. One
cannot help but be struck by the similarity between
Sandinista attitudes toward religious life and the goals of
the German Christian movement. Faith is ideology. The
Kingdom of God is the revolution. What else can be concluded from the various statements of Sandinista leaders?
In a statement concerning an attempt to refashion the
celebration of Christmas, they seek "to make it a special
day for the children, one with a different content, fundamentally political." Playing upon the words of 1 John 4:20,
they state that "the only way to love God, whom we do not
see, is by contributing to the advancement of this revolutionary process in the most sensible and radical way possible. Only then shall we be loving our brothers, whom we
do see." Among the Sandinistas, to be a Christian is to be
a revolutionary! "The true Christians, the sincere Christians, embrace the option of the Sandinista revolution."[17]
True Christianity lies in unquestioning support of the party
and revolution. Belli notes the closed circle of acceptable
faith and the intent to strangle any religious expression
transcendent of *sandinismo* by calling attention to the
"Document of the 72 Hours," which states Sandinista strategies for the exercise of power. In regard to the churches,
the document carries the ominous tones of Germany in
the 1930s:

> With the Catholic and Evangelical church, we should
> foster relations at the diplomatic level, observing a
> careful policy that seeks how to neutralize, as far as
> possible, the conservative stands and how to increase
> the links with priests open to the revolution, at the
> same time that we promote the revolutionary sectors
> of the church. With the Protestant church . . . we
> should implement a restrictive policy developing intel-
> ligence surveillance on them, and, if they are caught
> off guard, expel them at once.[18]

Utilizing the "liberation theology" so fashionable in some church circles, the Sandinistas stressed the notion that every act or affirmation, or absence thereof, is a politically charged action. Therefore, church bodies could be held in contempt or be regarded as subversive merely as a result of their remaining neutral in regard to political issues. "It is important to note that failure to 'embrace the option of the Sandinista revolution' need not involve explicit rejection or criticism of the revolution. It might mean merely the failure to explicitly support the revolution."[19]

In Sandinista Nicaragua, the revolutionary vanguard posited itself as the embodiment of "the people." Therefore, to oppose them or even to refuse to acknowledge their ultimacy was to prove oneself an enemy, not only of the political leadership, but of Christ Himself. The extent to which the gospel had been politicized is seen in such "hymns" as composed for revolutionary churches by the FSLN as "Jesus Has Been Born in Palacaguina." In this song, Mary contemplates Jesus' future as a carpenter while Jesus envisions his future as a guerrilla fighter! Or consider a baptismal ceremony in which "Original Sin" is identified as the "division of society into classes" and where a rite of exorcism is invoked identifying the unclean spirits of "egoism, capitalism, and Somocismo," after which water is poured out on the child, indicating the reception of revolutionary membership.[20]

Artwork in churches also revealed the transformation of Christian salvation into political ideology. In Managua, revolutionary priests ministered at one church in which

the altar was backed by a large mural depicting the Nicaraguan boy Christ flanked by fathers and mothers of revolutionary martyrs, liberated women, and tables of food
symbolic of the heaven-on-earth promised through revolutionary struggle. Another mural depicted revolutionary
martyrs Carlos Fonseca and Augusto Sandino with the
Sandinista flag. The red and black of the flag symbolized
death and the "resurrection" that the revolution brings.[21]

One would think that such activities and symbols would
have earned the universal protest of Nicaraguan Christians, Catholic and Protestant alike, to say nothing of interested church communities here in the United States.
And, in truth, there were courageous voices raised, most
notably that of Managuan Archbishop Cardinal Obando y
Bravo. Sadly, however, broad sections of contemporary
Christianity proved to have learned little from the previous experience of the German church struggle. The
Sandinista politicization of "Christ" was uncritically supported by numerous church organizations. Among those
cited by Belli are such ecumenical centers as the Centro
Antonio Valdivieso (CAV), Jesuit groups such as the
Instituto Historico Centroamericano (IHCA) and the
Centro de Promocion Agraria (CEPA), Eje Ecumenico
(MEC-CELADEC), and the Protestant Centro de Promocion
y Desarrollo (CEPAD). These groups were, and continue
to be, deeply involved in programs to meet the physical
needs of the Nicaraguan people but were virtually silent in
regard to governmental abuses of human rights. On occasion, individual representatives even applauded Sandinista
harassment of non-compromised elements of Nicaraguan
Christianity.

Indeed, a central task of Christian thought in the
present day is to clarify and maintain the identity of Jesus
Christ in the face of various streams of "creative" theology. Besides the politicized "Christ" evidenced in such
movements as the Sandinista front, we are presently seeing the concepts of "God" and "Christ" reduced to mere
subjective symbols, what Francis Schaeffer called "conno-
tation words," standing for little more than personal whims

and feelings. Although Jesus taught his followers to think of God as Father, a recent conference sponsored by two major denominations of Protestantism adopted feminine images of God in celebrations approaching goddess worship. The conference, entitled "RE-Imagining: A Global Theological Conference by Women," represented to its supporters "cutting edge" theology and referred to God by the name of Sophia, a feminine word for wisdom. In a panel discussion on the subject of Jesus, a professor from Union Theological Seminary in New York (an institution forever on the "cutting edge" of theology, whatever the current "edge" happens to be!) strongly implied the unnecessary presence of doctrine in favor of a simple sensitivity "to the God within." In a closing "worship" service, prayers were addressed to "our sweet Sophia," seemingly for purposes of exalting women as the image of God. The ceremony called attention to women who, with their warm body fluids, "remind the world of its pleasures and sensations."[22] Did the participants realize, one wonders, how similar such "theology" is to the German Fascist doctrine of divinity, as set forth by Ernst Bergmann's catechism for "Positive Christianity," an intriguing document in which we learn that "the living world is the womb of the high human mind," and that "the All-Mother gives birth to Knowing, Being, and Mind." Bergmann might have felt right at home at the RE-Imagining conference of today's Presbyterians and Methodists! "We speak of a modern nature religion when we speak of the Mind-child God, who lives in the womb of the All-Mother."[23]

Related to the problem of language is the contemporary loss of integrity in educational processes. That there is a deep sense of impending crisis linked to declining educational standards was demonstrated in the surprising and overwhelming public response to Allan Bloom's 1988 best-seller *The Closing of the American Mind*. The book's subtitle, "How Higher Education Has Failed Democracy and Impoverished the Souls of Today's Students," could apply equally to educational processes all along the way, from elementary to high school to college. What Bloom identified so cogently was our culture's growing decay of confidence in its own intellectual, artistic, and political heritage. Since his book appeared, other similar works by Page Smith, Dinesh d' Souza, Charles Sykes, Thomas Sowell, and others have refined the picture of educational crisis, and a virtual warfare has emerged in academic circles over matters of curriculum "core studies." Suddenly, the standing heritage in history, political thought, and literature must defend itself in the face of trendy specialties (often rooted in racial considerations) that trivialize intellectual life and rob students of a deserved sense of rootedness in the cultural milieu of which they are a part. These controversies carry much weight in defining the lines of today's "culture war," and one of the more unsettling parallels between our own social reality and that of Germany during the thirties is the significant energy displayed by those who, in essence, hate and seek to delegitimize their own society. Unable to live with the inevitable imperfections that attend any cultural tradition, radical academic armies marching under the various banners of "diversity," "multiculturalism," "feminism," and other trendy causes attack not only the flaws of Western democracy, but scorn even its best and highest achievements.

What are the tasks of education, and why does today's situation in America give evidence of a potential social disaster in the not too distant future?

Certainly, one of the foundational goals of education is to communicate a sense of what is true and valuable, both in terms of the universal aspects of the human condition and in relation to one's own cultural heritage. To fail in this task is to generate the kind of cultural despair that can set the stage for any meaning structure that can plausibly offer its vision to masses of people. One thing is certain. A society that regularly inculcates, through its educational institutions, scorn for its own heritage and institutions through outright vilification or programmed ignorance is setting itself up for easy subversion of its spiritual and moral foundations.

Educationally, the seeds have been planted for the realization of some of the worst scenarios of science-fiction anti-utopian novels. Consider, for example, the emergence over the past forty years of one of the more prominent imaginary characters to appear on the American scene—"Johnny." Johnny, of course, is the catch-name and symbol of the young child who can't do anything. Johnny can't read. Johnny can't write. Johnny can't count.

Which all means, of course, that Johnny can't think. And, increasingly, Johnny cannot remember. He has lost historical memory, a loss that is at a crisis point and which was of such concern that the situation energized Lynne V. Cheney, while serving as chair of the National Endowment for the Humanities, to publish the NEH study *American Memory* (1987), which outlined the marked decline in the teaching of history and literature in American public schools.

We value our traditions of representative government and the ideals of democracy. But, historically, democratic systems are rare. Can such systems be sustained in the absence of an understanding of their intellectual and spiritual roots? In a remarkable article published in *The Atlantic* and carrying the arresting title "Can We Be Good Without God?" author Glenn Tinder asks the question: "To what extent are we now living on moral savings accumulated over many centuries but no longer being replenished?" Tinder's thesis is a radical challenge to modern concepts of secular progress and illuminates the relationship between spiritual commitments and social reality. The human values that constitute so much of the motivation and goal of Western political life have been grounded in Judeo-Christian theism, but, once the source is negated, it is only a matter of time before the edifice crumbles. For Tinder, our position at the present time is "precarious."[24]

Increasingly, we see education giving way to little more than propaganda, and, with the decreasing levels of intellectual skills, there is a parallel inability to discern the difference. Leni Riefenstahl's image-making genius on behalf of Adolf Hitler has now passed on its techniques to American society and is regularly practiced in the political sphere, as advertising agents emerge as the necessary front-line troops in election campaigns. Today, one slick television ad of thirty seconds duration can outshine any number of well-crafted, thoughtful speeches (which is perhaps why we don't see very many of the latter anymore).

As we look at the national educational scene, it is almost as if we have lost the ability to educate in any true sense, and, hence, the substitution of bogus disciplines and goals is increasingly on the rise. We can detect this at all levels, and, in some extreme cases, it constitutes nothing less than a frontal assault on the mind itself. The current vigor of debate over "core curriculum" issues reveals a significant number of educators who would seem to deny that there is anything that is actually basic to education—an attitude that expresses itself in meaningless, random course offerings constituting the academic "cafeteria." This is not just another academic option, a way of organizing a curriculum in the interest of student freedom of choice. The implications of such arrangements are profound. What can one conclude other than that nothing is more important than anything else, that nothing is more basic or fundamental, and that everything is of equal value? The result is the trivialization of learning into a do-your-own-thing academic libertinism that gives equal status to contemporary popular writers and Shakespeare and which presents the student with one overriding academic goal— "Career Potential."

There is a macabre scene in the 1978 television mini-series movie "Holocaust." One of the central characters, a Nazi bureaucrat, is brought into the work of "special handling"—a Nazi euphemism for mass extermination of undesirables. As this young man begins to discuss his work with his wife and communicates some unease over it (the remaining vestiges of moral conscience), his wife vigorously encourages him to work harder and protect his position. After all, it is his career that is at stake! Who knows how high he might rise through responsibilities carried out with force and "excellence"?

Farfetched for America? Perhaps not. Where does the potential for such callousness in the interests of success begin? Clearly, it starts at whatever point a moral choice is to be made that may bump up against perceived self-interest. It is no secret that one of the most serious and pervasive problems in the educational world today is cheating, and not just by students. The realm of academic research as carried out by professors is afflicted as well as student life, where between 40 and 90 percent of college students commit some form of academic dishonesty, according to studies published in the *Journal of College Student Development*. These behaviors, undertaken amidst pressures to prove competence through high grades, are the first indicators of other and more serious implications for the future. Success through disregard for truth has no ending point. In the final analysis, Nazi bureaucrats who conducted the "final solution" were seeking advancement and commendation to the point that they could convince themselves that they were dealing with an abstract problem rather than with real human beings. The principle is no different for a student who hires another person to take a test or who submits an A research paper picked from a fraternity file. Reality is willfully, consciously distorted in the interest of "career." In this regard, the careerist mentality that has taken American higher education by storm over the past decade is proving to be deep, rich fertilizer for a replay of fascism's most tragic and pathetic scenarios—the "ordinary" acts of evil carried out by "ordinary" individuals in pursuit of the "ordinary" comforts of life.

At elementary and secondary levels, there is growing visibility of programs that actually constitute the substitution of propaganda and subtle indoctrination for education. This is no more prominently evident than in the area of so-called social studies where such true disciplines as history have been absorbed, diluted, or simply dumped aside in the interests of "peace studies," "global education," environmentalism, various programs related to "stress reduction," and racialist-ethnic programs in "self-esteem." The stated goals of such programs are difficult to argue against, as they are always stated in terms of widely recognized virtues: peace on earth, cooperation and understanding among diverse people, a clean environment, control of destructive impulses, and so forth.

But, we should have learned by now that noble sounding, worthy goals are easily stated to attract an audience and are especially effective with naive, gullible listeners. It is not without reason that Christ warned of "wolves who come to you in sheep's clothing." One does not need to dig too far in modern history to notice a Reign of Terror in the name of "Liberty, Equality, Fraternity," or a swastika-banded antichrist promising a spiritually hungry people "positive Christianity!" Educational programs promising to educate young minds for utopia are at the very least stupid and naive, governed by the discredited notion of human perfectibility. At their worst, such programs constitute nothing less than a frontal attack on the intellect itself.

Take, for example, studies in "peace." The very suggestion that there is a discipline that can legitimately be called "peace studies" is in and of itself a clue that the proponents have fallen prey to the disease of "euphemism-itis" or bottom line anti-intellectualism. We live in a day when almost anything can be made into an instant discipline of academic research (the latest such bogus discipline is in the form of "Leadership" curricula). But, if there is any doubt as to the propagandist intents and methods of this form of "education," all one has to do is listen to the rhetoric of its proponents and peruse the "curriculum" materials.

It turns out that "peace studies" is little more than mindless exhortation, aimed at young and forming minds, to avoid any sort of conflict, personal or societal. Politically, such programs enshrine suspicion toward national traditions and national defense while promulgating an uncritical acceptance of a centralized world government—in other words, a global totalitarian state.

The apparent goal of such "educational" programs is to create a society of passive, pacifistic individuals motivated by sentimental feelings rather than by thought. This is evident in the way they treat history itself. A social studies text used in Lincoln, Nebraska, for example, treats World War II as a tragic example of man's love of weapons and does not even mention Hitler's plans of genocide! Hence, world-shaping events are reduced to simplistic explanation. There are too many weapons, and all human problems can be solved by doing away with them. On the basis of such "educational materials," young boys and girls are supposed to legitimately speculate on how to make a safer and more peaceful world. In some curriculum materials, students are encouraged to think in terms of centralized global government through such exercises as designing a flag for the world, the purpose being to develop allegiance to the world rather than to local or national culture. That the Judeo-Christian heritage is the marked "bad boy" in the plot of world difficulties is seen in notes given in teachers' guides, where it is suggested that instructors point out the destructive impact of the concept of "chosenness" in religions and mark Christianity as an "especially war-like religion."[25] Nationwide, such curriculum materials make use of John Lennon's song "Imagine," which constitutes a secular eschatology in which "religion" (i.e., Christian theism) is banished and where there are "no possessions" either. Just the reality of the whole world as "one." No conflict. Nothing to take a stand for, or against. Nothing to strive for. Just "peace." Heaven on earth, populated with perfected humanity. Here, propaganda is merged with outright hypocrisy. There are few things more contradictory than John Lennon, a millionaire who guarded his fortune for his own use and comfort, singing about the virtues of a society in which there are no possessions.

The danger in all this is clear when we recall how readily modern totalitarian societies refer to brain-washing programs as "re-education." It is frightful that the educational system of the world's beacon of political and spiritual freedom should be inculcating the very same distortion.

In the early seventies, singer and songwriter Barry McQuire recorded a song called "The Eve of Destruction." If we are on the eve of destruction, the various ingredients are overt as well as subtle. Added to the concerns already noted is a pervasive cultural despair that afflicts virtually everything. And, there are signs that even Liberals, known for ethical relativism and "openness" toward just about everything, are getting concerned. The situation was noted in a surprising article published by the editors of *The New Republic*, 8 February 1988, entitled "The Culture of Apathy." The writers remark that liberal culture has reached a crisis and that the liberal mentality is lost in a "fog bank of insouciance" born of modern liberalism's licentiousness concerning every form of pursuit and gratification. No one is safe in this "culture of lassitude," and they see a new barbarism arising that expresses itself not only in crime and violence, but in a general degradation of life that is "actively encouraged by our popular culture and propagated by the incessant images of our mass media, that nothing is true and everything is permitted."[26]

The crisis in "liberalism," according to the authors, is its inability to respond to moral decline owing to the very nature of the ideology. Liberals are left cold to the question of cultural decadence precisely because the situation challenges their own "attachment to the endlessness of personal freedoms." Liberals are fully invested, intellectually and psychologically, in "the doctrine of ever-expanding rights" of "everyone to everything"—including pornographers and criminals—and any suggestion of the negative consequences seems a threat to the liberal idea itself. Much will depend on whether they can muster enough intellectual courage "to stop averting their eyes."

The swamp of ethical relativism has led to a quicksand bed for an entire civilization. It was thought to lead to freedom. Yet, strange as it may seem, the actual evidence is that ethical relativism leads instead to tyranny. The reason for this is that in relativism there is no end; there are no limits that can legitimately be appealed to in case of a society out of moral control. The ideology does not permit it. But, people have to live and will continue to value the safety of their persons and possessions. If the internal moral sense of a people, that which allows for reasoned social interaction, is diminished to an adequate extent throughout the society, the logical desire will be for force, a tyranny of order born of the soil of fear. What will people opt for when the situation is extreme enough? Order at any price. Meaning of any kind. A structure of meaning and order that itself becomes the only absolute, enforced by the state. But, as Jean-Francois Revel has stated, "only in the totalitarian society does the state arrogate to itself the right to give 'meaning' to people's lives,"[27] and University of Chicago professor Leszek Kolakowski, in a *New Republic* article, warns of "the danger that our civilization may collapse into nihilistic sluggishness and become an easy prey for tyranny."[28] Kolakowski sees in contemporary American society an alarming erosion of the "status of human personality," consequently diminishing "both the concept of personal responsibility and the feeling of it." Realizing the kind of disjunction between language and reality we have noted above, Kolakowski asks the question: "If 'I' am not 'I,' if the word 'I' is a pronoun to which no reality—at least no morally constituted reality—corresponds,. . . then indeed there is no reason why 'I,' rather than the abstraction 'society,' should be responsible for anything." For Kolakowski, the assignment of primary reality status to "society," while diminishing our ability to assert the separate and irreducible status of individual personality, "makes us conceptually defenseless in the face of totalitarian doctrines, ideologies, and institutions."[29]

There is some evidence, however, that we are seeing a move in America today to follow the idolatrous illusion of political salvation as various voices raise the rhetoric of a "politics of meaning." The most notable sounds in the chorus come from First Lady Hillary Rodham Clinton, who, in her younger years, aspired to see government take on the task of "human reconstruction," and who now looks for "a new definition of civil society which answers the unanswerable questions" of how to develop a society that "fills us up . . . and makes us feel that we are part of something bigger than ourselves." One of Mrs. Clinton's ardent supporters, her former pastor Don Jones, has given

a recommendation that strikes ominous chords. Jones sees
her as a person who "realizes absolutely the truth of the
human condition, which is that you cannot depend on the
basic nature of man to be good and you cannot depend
entirely on moral suasion to make it good. You have to
use force."[30]

Leon Wieseltier comments that the First Lady's project
constitutes "a spiritual expectation of politics," composed
of an "organic mood, a faith in feeling as a guide to
political action" and a conviction that officials are teachers, carrying out a governmental mandate to make sure
that people are "good." It all sounds uncomfortably familiar, given the history of the twentieth century, and, in
Wieseltier's estimation, "the righteousness of the Clintons
is a little creepy."[31]

Wieseltier's analysis of the social righteousness of Bill
and Hillary Clinton is fascinating and reads like a refresher
course on German Fascist slogans. He locates the roots of
their transformational vision in the thinking of the influential management consultant W. Edwards Deming and
his disciples. Deming's writings pulsate with denunciations
of individual merit and emphasize the subordination of
individuals to the overall necessity of "cooperation." In a
passage reminiscent of the Nazi slogan of "Strength
Through Joy," Deming envisions a utopia in which "there
will be joy in work, joy in learning," as everyone operates
in a cooperative manner with everyone else and in which
competition for individual reward has vanished. The key
to all this, however, is Deming's cult of the leader.
Wieseltier's estimate of this principle is that Deming's
theories constitute a "cold demand for a concentration of
power at the top" in a leader who "possesses knowledge,
personality, and persuasive power." Deming admirer Robert B. Reich, secretary of labor, declares his own belief in
"collective entrepreneurialism" and the death of "the myth
of the Triumphant Individual."[32] Hear the words of another leader, who had similar thoughts! In describing the
constructive powers of the super Aryan man, Adolf Hitler
held that the building up of a culture "essentially depends

on the readiness of the individual to renounce his own personal opinions and interests and to lay both at the service of the human group. . . . The renunciation of one's own life for the sake of the community is the crowning significance of the idea of all sacrifice."[33] Hitler, Deming, Reich, and the Clintons would seem to all agree in calling this "idealism."

The illusion of political salvation is necessarily tied in to the subject of leadership. There is a crisis in leadership, manifesting itself in widespread distrust and ridicule of public officials, revelations of moral misconduct in spiritual leaders, to say nothing of the normal, everyday deadness of spirit afflicting a bureaucratic social structure governed by the singular and pervasive value of "efficiency." A twin spectre arises out of this milieu. On the one hand, we may observe a dullness of spirit in regard to leaders in general, the kind of apathy that encourages blind obedience to "the system," however it may be constituted for individuals in their particular walks of life. On the other hand, there is the vulnerability born of this cultural despair, a vulnerability to the deceits of any sufficiently charismatic leader who seems to act with vision and authority. Cynicism and moral relativism, side by side with the human hunger for legitimate and inspiring leadership, are volatile ingredients of a gathering darkness.

Utopian dreams attract many, be they expressed through narrow cults or grand visions of a "New World Order." Sociologist Zygmunt Bauman of the University of Leeds has argued that the fundamental character of modern, bureaucratic, "efficient" civilization was the necessary condition for such an event as the Holocaust. Although the past reveals its episodes of mass murders, pogroms, and brutal dislocations of populations, the Holocaust has a distinctly modern flavor in the linkage between modern genocide and the efficient pursuit of the grand vision of a better and radically different society. Modern genocide is, argues Bauman, "an element of social engineering" tied to the goal of conforming human beings to the pre-envisioned design of a perfect society. Here, we see clearly the intrinsic relationship of utopianism to tyranny, for the managers of modern genocide were precisely those dedicated to societal "perfection." Genocide proceeds, says Bauman, from the ambition to remake society so as to conform to an overall plan that represents an aesthetic ideal built to "standards of superior beauty."[34]

The lessons of the Holocaust must be studied, writes Bauman, precisely because we live in the very type of society that made it possible in the first place, and which was morally disarmed from preventing it. It is a world of utopian visions wedded to technological power, along with a bureaucratic numbing of courage and a sense of truth, and a mounting cultural despair awaiting a regenerating "messiah," be it a person or a movement or both. The "Angel of Light" awaits a return to center stage.

Page Smith has likewise noted parallels between our times and the years that built toward the Holocaust. In *Killing the Spirit*, a study of the spiritual vacuum in today's institutions of higher education, he calls attention to the attraction of sophisticated, intellectually accomplished westerners to the extremes of irrational, cultic dictatorships. Left in a spiritual void created by the fashionable rejection of Jesus Christ and the biblical worldview and facing the abyss of meaninglessness that is secular humanism, they are "eventually led into large and in some instances frighteningly powerful groups, full-blown cults invariably led by a single charismatic 'teacher.' "[35] Study of the professional backgrounds of the followers of the Bhagwan Shree Rajneesh, for example, revealed that the vast majority had attended college and had earned degrees, with a significant percentage (12 percent) claiming Ph.D.s from respected American institutions. This disturbing spectacle, writes Smith, is a direct result of a society that has disengaged from its meaning structures while providing no viable alternative objects of belief and comfort. Hence, an illness that, in its extreme, leaves even talented, accomplished, and intelligent men and women vulnerable to the sad absurdity of an old man claiming to be a god. "They took up with the devil, in the deceptive form of an old Indian wise man."[36]

In the emerging New Age movement, such hysteria threatens to turn the entire world into a mass, devilish cult on a universal basis. Rooted in the same occultism that moved through the Nazi ideology, this radical social force holds out for increasing numbers a future hope of world unity and a human breakthrough in evolution to "higher consciousness." In recent years, the movement (NAM) has generated much critical literature, both secular and Christian, and such critiques have touched upon the relationships between its outlook and the very ideology that formed the basis of nazism. Although the vast majority of people identifying themselves with the NAM would be appalled at such connections, it is appropriate to take note of some primary aspects of this current form of irrationality within the context of post-Holocaust reflections.

The New Age is the most recent form of utopianism to capture the imagination of Europe and America. As in all utopian visions, it criticizes the present imperfect social reality (the real environment) from the standpoint of a perfect but nonexistent reality. Previous utopian visions of modern times such as the French Revolution, communism, and nazism have inevitably sought to establish themselves through the practice of "cleansing" the new society of all its old, unwanted elements and "outworn" values. We have no reason to believe that the New Age vision is any different. And, why should it be so? The very nature of a utopian dream is to purge away anything or anybody that is not fully in accord with the fundamental premises of its plan of social harmony. Advancing "harmony" as the prime value of social life, utopias build a logical, inexorable basis for the persecution or extermination of whatever realities, ideas, or impulses threaten that harmony. But, harmony is not really the concept that defines the utopia, although it is a positive sounding term likely to generate emotional conviction and loyalty to the vision. In actuality, conformity is the real glue of the society, the kind of conformity that results not from shared values or an overall sense of responsibility to God and other people,

but from the necessity to purge away all traces of individuality, creativity, or even desire. A fictional interpretation
of this condition was presented by Ayn Rand in her short,
anti-utopian romance *Anthem*, which expresses the terror
of a society in which even the concept of individual identity, symbolized by the concept "I," has been banished.
Although Rand was not a Christian, she vigorously upheld
the reality of individuals and the necessity of personal,
rational consciousness in human life. Without such recognition, no terror or brutality could be held back. It is
interesting to note, in relation to the New Age movement,
the exact premise underlying the totalitarian state in Rand's
novel—the nonreality of the individual. In the New Age, all
is one, and, therefore, all individual identity is illusory. It
is not too difficult to imagine that, in a politically realized
New Age, affirmation of individual identity through independent thought and action could conceivably be
criminalized.

Consider, for example, the implications inherent in
the vision of New Age writer Peter Russell, author of *The
Global Brain*. Russell envisions the entire world as a "su-
perorganism" constituted by a harmonized consciousness
distributed over the face of the entire planet earth, comprised of each and every individual of the human race.[37]
Although Russell anticipates the objection that individuality may be obliterated in such a system, he insists on a
premise that is essentially Fascist—that the sole justification for individual diverse expression is the degree to
which it makes a contribution to the whole. For this to
happen, however, there must be "a coming together of
minds" through the "evolution of consciousness," a development that will bring forth a lifeform "as far beyond us
as we are beyond single cells," a kind of superconsciousness
happening at the planetary level. His model for imagining
this is a photograph composed of many dots in which the
significant reality is in the whole.[38] Russell, however, is not
content to allow "evolution" to take its own course in its
own time, and, in this matter, he is typical of New Age
believers. The situation of planetary crisis is urgent, and it

falls upon humanity to help the evolutionary process along by changing fundamental assumptions underlying human thought and behavior. His utopianism waxes strong as he calls, evangelistically, for "a new world view" that is "holistic, nonexploitive, ecologically sound, long-term, global, peaceful, humane, and cooperative."[39]

Naturally, New Age people are vitally interested in all aspects of society that might be employed to develop the proper form of consciousness, most notably education and government. But, the realm of business is also a large field of NAM activity. As people (lacking proper consciousness) have become aware of consciousness-manipulating "counselors," "consultants," "educators," and "leaders," controversies have arisen throughout the country in schools, corporations, and small businesses that have seen students and employees pressured to "develop consciousness." More ominous than many people realize is the developing requirement of "community service" in schools, where students face the irrational and contradictory notion of required "voluntary" service! In the business world, we are seeing perhaps the first indications of the NAM's utopian mechanisms of "cleansing" as individuals lose their jobs through non-cooperation in "consciousness development" sessions.[40]

Ultimately, the NAM's vision is world unity under the authority of a world government, an ideal that explains much concerning New Agers' enthusiasm for "peace" and the instrumentalities of the United Nations. Although New Age plans for world peace and government assume the establishment of a worldwide liberal democracy, a more critical view sees in all this the open invitation to a tyranny that an Adolf Hitler would envy. Some New Age leaders see the world as coming to acquiesce to a world government out of simple concern for survival, as regional and ethnic conflicts explode in various places. Walter Berns, writing in a *National Review* article, has defined a likely scenario of such a development. A world government would have to be armed, he observes, but moreover it would have to see to it that no one else was armed and that no individual state had retained arms. This condition alone "would demand verification . . . and verification would require a police force authorized to search and seize at will. . . . It would almost certainly be, it would have to be, a tyranny of global proportion."[41] But, he makes the more telling observation that, in such an arrangement, there could be no separation of Church and State. The ruler must, of necessity, be head of both. "He will be like a god—Orwell gave him (or it) the name of 'Big Brother.' "[42] The significance of Berns' critique can be appreciated in view of the language of exalted praise that New Age leaders give to the United Nations. Sri Chinmoy, a meditation leader at the U.N., has stated that the organization is nothing less than "the chosen instrument of God," a "divine messenger carrying the banner of God's inner vision and outer manifestation." For Chinmoy, the United Nations is the very soul of the world, a soul that "is all-loving, all-nourishing, and all-fulfilling."[43] Along a similar vein, Robert Muller offers the view that in the United Nations "all human knowledge, concerns, efforts and aspirations converge."[44] Lest readers dismiss such comments as so much fanciful extremism, it bears noting that United Nations armed forces are active today in dozens of political theaters around the world and that increasingly national sovereignty is being sacrificed to its authority.

The history of modern times amply demonstrates the horrible realities of utopian visions once they gain political power. The French Revolution was the first terrible example of man's attempt to forge a "new age" or society inherited by a "new" humanity purged of all traces of undesired older traditions. One is struck by the parallels between the French revolutionary vision of the late eighteenth century and today's New Age consciousness. Historian James Billington, in *Fire in the Minds of Men*, has noted that the root of the revolution was a belief in secular salvation in which the present world was hell and revolutionary activity a kind of collective purgatory leading to a future paradise on earth. "History itself would provide the final judgement" through a totally new and entirely man-made order. Billington defines the "faith of our time" as utopian revolutionism, originally rooted in the French movement that, as we all know, found its culmination in the appropriately named "Reign of Terror."

> Modern revolutionaries are believers, no less committed and intense than were the Christians or Muslims of an earlier era. What is new is the belief that a perfect secular order will emerge from the forcible overthrow of traditional authority. This inherently implausible idea gave dynamism to Europe in the nineteenth century, and has become the most successful ideological export of the West to the world in the twentieth.[45]

The French experience combined a noble slogan—"Liberty, Equality, Fraternity"—with a rising tide of violence against any and all nonconformity to the vision of a "new age" humanity. This pattern was repeated in communism and nazism. Why should anyone think that today's New Age utopianism will be any different, especially in view of the movement's radical ethical relativism and consequent failure to distinguish any basis for discernment between good and evil?

In fact, one sees every classic symptom of an emergent totalitarianism in today's New Age movement. Defining totalitarianism as "utopianism come to power," Jeane Kirkpatrick has offered a description of these symptoms and principles. Totalitarian movements seek the complete transformation of culture through purposive social engineering and thought reform and set forth goals that constitute the destiny of some collectivity rather than the aspirations of concrete persons. In fact, "totalitarian utopians attribute no independent or intrinsic value or reality to individuals." The end of history and collective destiny is the reigning, empowering vision. "The totalitarian is not interested in tinkering, in piecemeal resolution of problems, but in final solutions."[46]

Kirkpatrick's reflections weigh heavily when one contemplates the implications of aggressive New Age curricula in American public education and the statements of some of its leading voices to the effect that the New Age will have no place for the unfit. Certainly, the movement's doctrine of the universal "godhood" of humanity, recognition of which defines "proper" consciousness, will of necessity regard all traces of traditional Judeo-Christian theism as "false" consciousness. What bizarre final solutions will be offered as "cleansing" measures in the New Age that we are told is coming upon us now?

Indeed, the New Age movement is nothing less than a new statement of racist utopianism, inasmuch as the development of a new "consciousness" defines the emergence of a new race of super-humanity. This fundamental aspect of the New Age is often lost amidst all of the various forms and expressions that the movement takes. Yet, I believe it is the essence of the whole thing. It is Nietszche all over again, the continuing voice of antichrist.

Racism, as a basis for a New Age, is made clear in the writings of the seminal thinkers of the "new consciousness." One such "prophet" was Richard Maurice Bucke, a Canadian psychiatrist who, after experiencing an inner illumination in 1873, wrote his classic work *Cosmic Consciousness*. His fundamental vision informs today's New Age movement in proposing that the human race, as presently constituted, is but a transitional form of life out of which a new race is evolving, a premise found in contemporary New Age writers such as John Randolph Price. It is clear from such writings that in the future certain people will be as far above present humanity as present human beings are above animals. The key to this elevation is a kind of "consciousness" that destroys the sense of sin, shame, and "the sense of good and evil as contrasted one with the other."[47] Although historically present in only a few special individuals, Bucke saw that "step in promotion" (consciousness) as awaiting a manifestation in the whole race, with a time coming in which individuals without the higher consciousness will be seen as bearing "a mark of inferiority parallel to the absence at present of the moral nature"—in other words, like lower animals.

What such a vision would come to in the hands of a

Hitler, Bucke could not have known or anticipated at the time his book was originally written. The same cannot be said, however, for John Randolph Price, who apparently is untroubled by the parallels between the rhetoric that led to the Holocaust and his own references to emerging "Superbeings" who are by nature and action a stark contrast to ordinary mortals, a population he refers to as a "polluted mass" existing "completely out of the stream of Truth."[48]

The inevitable question, of course, is what happens in the New Age to all the "lower beings" among us, the ones without a moral nature and who have "no share in the stream of Truth." There is no reason to conclude that New Age utopianism, should it actually achieve widespread political expression, will be any different in its effects than other utopias of modern life, be they of the Left or the Right. Clearly, creatures that have no share in the stream of truth, or whose level of consciousness disqualifies them from citizenship, live outside the spectrum of moral commitment.

Zigmunt Bauman makes a compelling connection between modern genocide and the concept of society as a garden, in which parts of the social habitat are defined as human "weeds." "Modern genocide," he writes, "is a gardener's job. . . . If garden design defines its weeds, there are weeds wherever there is a garden. And weeds are to be exterminated." The social project is to create and maintain society as a perfect garden. Human beings who are designated as "unfit" are, like all other weeds, objects to be segregated, contained, prevented from spreading, and kept outside the mainstream. "If all these means prove insufficient, they must be killed."[49] Bauman's image is intriguing, especially in view of New Age ecological concepts of the earth as a living organism evolving in total consciousness, purging itself of unhealthy elements. For Bauman, modern social organization is more than capable of genocide. What it needs, though, is a trigger. And, that trigger can be provided by nothing more than impatience and fear about present social conditions combined with a bold vision of a better society that is, according to some accepted criterion, "pure" of familiar troublesome failings.

Odd as it may seem, the potential for a repetition of the Holocaust resides as much in human idealism as in blatant cruelty or hatred. That such a potential resides within the New Age movement is not generally recognized, notwithstanding the alarm bells that were rung by Detroit attorney Constance Cumbey, who, in her book *The Hidden Dangers of the Rainbow*, first alerted the Christian world to the nature of this "alternative altar." Not everyone accepts Cumbey's endtimes scenario or her conspiracy outlook, but one does not have to in order to appreciate the curious historic parallels between New Age thought and the violent utopian revolutions of modern times. One need only look to history to see that the social transformation rhetoric of our day is simply another version of older foundations of terror. The regeneration of mankind, the creation of a new humanity by human means, leads with a cruel logic to mass extermination as all moral distinctions are lost except those between the acknowledged "new" species and those who are not recognized as such. This is made clear by Ralph C. Hancock, writing in *Policy Review* in an article reflecting on the bicentennial of the French Revolution. The new human beings to be created through the revolution would be free of the characteristic limitations and failings that earlier generations had assumed to be rooted in the human condition. "Such a creation clearly requires a radical repudiation of the beliefs, habits, and institutions of the past; these must be destroyed in order to allow the emergence of regenerate humanity. The logic of the Terror follows from this radical project of destroying the past and creating a new humanity."[50]

At issue today is a short but profound question: What view of human nature will form the patterns of life in the decades ahead? A further question confronts Christians worldwide: How may we discern the truth, that it may govern our acts and allegiance?

Human life as evolutionary ascent lies at the root of destructive utopianism, New Age or otherwise. "Man," Adolf Hitler said to Hermann Rauschning, "has to be passed and surpassed. . . . Man is God in the making. Man has eternally to strain at his limitations. The moment he relaxes and contents himself with them, he decays and falls below the human level. He becomes a quasi-beast."[51] The centuries-old notion that humanity has no fixed nature but can evolve into a higher form under human direction combined with given natural forces, is diametrically opposed by the biblical revelation. Undeniably, though, the evolutionistic vision is a perceived hope of increasing attraction, especially as it becomes allied to genetic science that promises everything from genetically engineered cures for disease to cryonically achieved "eternal life." The prideful ecstasy proclaiming man as God has proved its staying power even through the devastations of the twentieth century and seems to gather force with the fast approach of a new millennium. It is the doctrine that sets the stone of an alternative altar for those who, for whatever reason, find God's revelation in Christ no longer compelling or credible. What will be the response of the Christian Church?

The signs are already about us that, as with national socialism, massive numbers of self-proclaimed Christians are willing and even eager to conform the "faith" to whatever new vision of society arises with enough power and imagination. It is not difficult to meet clergymen today who have a deeper sense of personal identification with secular humanists or New Agers than with Christians who accept such classical doctrines as the inspiration of Scripture and the uniqueness of God's incarnation in Jesus. Once again, as with Hitler, theology is being tied to the latest wind of modernity that blows sweet aromas of a fulfilled human future. Much depends, then, on how we understand who and what we are as creatures bearing the *Imago Dei*. Increasingly, the task of Christian preaching and apologetics will be to clarify the issue of human nature and to pose answers that will, like Elijah's challenge to the priests of Baal, prove the impotence of those altars presently being erected as monuments to the idol of Human Autonomy.

Memorials of the Holocaust are plentiful, and one of

the ironies of the practice is the persistent indictment of Christianity. Contradictions abound in this indictment. On the one hand, Christianity is charged with "causing" the Holocaust—a complaint lodged by Jews and Christians alike and readily accepted by ministers who, sad to say, seem to love guilt trips more than truth. But, alongside this indictment is the recognition that Christian witness is the world's best hope; the tragedy is its lack of discernment and slowness to speak and act. Implicitly, the attitude toward Christianity relative to the Holocaust seems to say "if the Church had only been what it is, in its truest sense, the great crime would have been impossible." The Body of Christ is tacitly acknowledged to be that power, that force capable of turning back the destructive tides of Nazi utopianism. Christian faith is seen to be Truth and Life by the very intensity of the indictment, as if to say "if you had been here this would not have happened."

Why should such a charge be leveled at an "irrelevant" tradition of the past? Why should such importance be attached to a perceived absence of involvement if the Christian Church is not, in fact, what Jesus declared it to be—the very salt of the earth and light of the world? There are, then, deep and persistent reasons for Christians to remember the Holocaust, not for reasons of an ongoing acceptance of a chic guilty conscience, but by way of applying in today's context the positive lessons to be learned from the Body of Christ that did stand and act. For in those actions resided the presence of Christ and the faith of His saints.

That the Bible, taken as the authoritative Word of God, is a bulwark against such crimes as the Holocaust is clearly demonstrated in the premises upon which the Confessing Church took its stance. Its power to restrain evil in the future is not lessened by the fact that the Church did not bring Hitler down. The point is, what enabled the Church to stand at all? One thing is clear. It was not "liberal" theology, or the Higher Criticism, or strained ideals of "Christ" as social transformation that gave the Church its ground for battle. William Hordern, in a pointed commentary on the career of Karl Barth, noted that Barth rejected the liberal theology in which he had been trained when he saw its ready accommodation to national socialism as the latest expression of progressive social transformation.[52]

The extent to which the Church in Germany retained its identity with "the faith once for all given to the saints" determined its ability to witness to the truth. A fundamental premise of this faith is the humbling doctrine of man's fallen nature and the radical distinction between God and the creature. So long as humanity subjects itself to the delusion that there is no such distinction to be made, giving ear to the lie of Eden, anything is possible.

There is a vital need today, as Holocaust memorials are observed, for Christians to think clearly about their faith in view of the Third Reich's shadow and to challenge the simplistic acceptance of a Christian collective guilt. If, after many centuries, the Church has rejected Medieval notions about the collective guilt of Jews for the death of Christ, can there now be acceptance of the same fallacy relative to Christianity and the Holocaust? The Church, while admitting and repenting of its past failures, must get on with the task of learning lessons from the experience that may prove instructive and strengthening for the future. At the core of this task is to appreciate and uphold the integrity of Christian confession and the biblical tradition.

The central presence of the Bible and its positive impact on culture, have been noted by Joshua O. Haberman, a rabbi in the reformed tradition of Judaism. Rabbi Haberman has written that America's "Bible Belt," contrary to the virulent scorn of its critics, is America's safety belt against a Holocaust happening here in the United States.[53] Haberman fled his native Vienna in 1938, just months after Austria came under the control of Nazi troops. Why was it that this cultured city succumbed to nazism without so much as even a mild resistance? Haberman calls attention to an intellectual climate "dominated by moral relativism, bordering on nihilism," that spiritually disarmed its people against the appeal of the pagan idolatry that was nazism. "As an eyewitness to the horror and barbarism of a totalitarian regime, I hold a different view of Americans who take the moral absolutes of the Bible seriously."[54]

For Rabbi Haberman, the Bible-believing people he met in the United States were in sharp contrast to the Austrian culture he had left behind. The sometimes uncouth, seemingly naive residents of Mobile, Alabama, offered a stark contrast to the outwardly sophisticated and courteous citizens of the Vienna he had known. Their roughness was balanced by qualities of openness and good-naturedness, whereas in Vienna he "was constantly on guard with people, wondering what reality might hide behind the mask of gracious courtesy." Of the Bible-belt people, he writes that "their Biblically grounded moral standards and faith in God, deeply rooted in and reinforced by all levels of society, acted as barriers against the excesses of governmental power that can lead to totalitarianism."

What, asks Haberman, made possible such despotisms as we have seen in the twentieth century? His answer is clear and forceful:

> The suspension of the Bible's moral "barriers" made possible all the atrocities of Hitler, Stalin, and other totalitarian rulers. It is no accident that the Soviet State and Hitler's Third Reich both identified the Bible and its teachers as primary enemies. . . . Rosenberg was not mistaken in judging the Bible to be incompatible with Nazi philosophy. The Bible mandates a Supreme Law, to which all human creatures, even the Führer, must submit. . . . On the whole, the official clerical leadership of German Protestantism and Catholicism left a dismal record of compromise, submission, and collaboration with the Nazi regime. Not so the members of the dissident Confessing Church . . . which, following Karl Barth's staunch fidelity to Scriptural theology, felt impelled to reject "unscriptural" Nazi views.[55]

As a Jew, Haberman acknowledges significant differences between himself and Bible-believing Christians concerning America's social agenda and public policy matters. Yet, overshadowing the differences is a common moral and spiritual vision growing from a recognition that the Bible gave the United States its moral vision that is the guarantor of fundamental rights and freedoms.

Whether or not the Bible and its moral vision constitutes a safety belt for a society in crisis depends, in the final analysis, on the degree to which its authority is acknowledged and accepted by a population. Until recent years, even those who rejected the inspiration and authority of Scripture, and who themselves were not even nominal Christians, nevertheless lived within and accepted what Francis Schaeffer called a "Christian consensus." The consensus, which expressed the general cultural impact of biblical morality and ethics, worked as a preservative "salt of the earth." The power of this consensus was seen in various ways, but a ready example would be the arena of popular culture, in which codes of speech and dialogue in literature and film omitted blasphemy and profane slang expressions. The consensus was also present in marriage customs, which inhibited divorce and criminalized adultery. The "salting" effect was evident in cultural products that severely limited profanity and explicit expression of sexual encounters and depictions of violence. Symbols of spiritual life such as ministers or priests were generally expressed in a positive manner, and the courageous, morally upright hero was in evidence.

Such conditions more or less held true through the decade of the 1950s but there are disturbing signs that now, in the 1990s, the salt has lost its power or that there is not enough of it left to go around. The language of violence, disgust, and insult pervades our arts to the extent that what was formerly marginal phenomena have now become mainstream. Conversations casually overheard in a library reading room or a public parking lot are likely to be sustained by the language of insult now trivialized by its very pervasiveness. For some this is freedom, but a parent writing in *Time* magazine's extensive article on popular culture (7 May 1990) poses a haunting question. In reference to an incident in which seven middle-class teens assaulted a mentally retarded girl to a watching audience of six friends, Charles Alexander asks, "Who knows what demons haunted the boys? Were they all psychologically disturbed, or were they acting *normally* in a culture where sexual violence is deemed tolerable, even entertaining [emphasis mine]?"[56]

In the attempts of contemporary society to remember the Holocaust, not nearly enough is done to actually confront the degree to which modern life and civilization present conditions that, in the right conjunction, could lead with cold logic to a repeat. At some risk, I will state here that perhaps too much focus is put on anti-Semitism as the one and only issue, the singular warning signal. If the Holocaust is to be remembered, its significance for humanity as a whole must be stressed, lest it become diminished to a parochial event in Jewish history. More focus is needed on the degree to which the principles of the "final solution" under nazism have been applied in more recent history to other peoples as well. Is not the world called to weep for Cambodians, for example, whose society was "cleansed" and "weeded" in similar fashion? Or, does remembrance of the Holocaust simply mean, in effect, "don't ever let this happen to us again," meaning Jews alone?

No doubt I risk the charge of anti-Semitism by even making such a suggestion. Yet, the Holocaust is not merely a Jewish event. Jewish people do not "own" the Holocaust. It is rather a universal paradigm of the kind of disaster that occurs when romantic utopian dreams are fused with modern corporate and political power in a spiritual vacuum that knows no sure word from God.

The Christian faith, expressed through the Body of Christ, remains as the only force on earth that can avert another Holocaust, as it is the custodian of God's revelation. As has often been observed, the key to any free society is the capacity of its people to practice self-governance. It is not, however, the bogus self-governance that makes every person a morally autonomous, self-affirmed god, but the kind that derives from a general recognition of an objective moral order and the reality of the Lawgiver who is above every so-called god, even the power of the state. The significance of theological doctrine, then, must never be lost upon the Church. Christ does not serve the human race exclusively through soup kitchens, clothing drives, and countless other manifestations of good works. What the Church should have learned from the Holocaust experience is that its capitulation to false theology, pretentious biblical criticism, and a confusion of God's kingdom with earthly political systems disarmed its entire mission and reason for being. National socialism was the most cleverly conceived and executed spiritual deception in history, playing upon religious images and even Christian terminology, while in reality serving a Satanic agenda. Churches today do not realize how dangerous is their all-too-frequent practice of courtesy toward all ideas and positions, their easy toleration of even the most outrageous theological "innovations."

The German church under nazism is indeed a paradigm that ought to instruct us concerning the consequences of lost doctrine. Weakened by a century of skeptical attacks upon the Scriptures and the confused acceptance of critics' conclusions by church leaders and seminaries, Christians were left to fish for themselves out of a theological lake of mere emotion in which no principles of spiritual discernment lived. The result was a hideous idolatry that fulfilled Peter's prophecy that "there will be false teachers among you, who will secretly bring in destructive heresies, even denying the Master who bought them, bringing upon themselves swift destruction" (2 Pet. 2:1). The task of interpreting the faith must never be confused with redefining it. The premise of all too many German intellectuals and theologians was that the modern age must dictate the content and meaning of Christian faith and that if doctrines of the historic faith were inconvenient to modern consciousness they must be thrown out. Jeffrey

Burton Russell's commentary on the modern liberal Christianity of the late nineteenth and early twentieth centuries carries an implicit warning about the Church's lust for worldly compatibility. He sees a Church embarrassed by its own beliefs, especially the supernatural framework of understanding reality. "Liberal Christians," he writes, "retreated, apologized, and adapted" to cultural trends until Christianity "all but lost its meaning." In "abandoning the independent epistemological bases of Christianity in experience, revelation, and tradition" they left themselves vulnerable to deception and destruction.[57]

Theologian Karl Barth, who led the movement known as Neo-Orthodoxy in response to seeing his theological colleagues and professors accommodating Christianity to nazism, realized that the manner and technique of Christian proclamation must change and adapt to cultural circumstances but that those realities must never dictate what is to be proclaimed. Culture may dictate and necessitate an approach of getting the Word of Christ out, but it can have nothing to say about matters of content.

The Holocaust witnesses to the awesome destructive potential of ordinary human beings through a confluence of spiritual deception, modern technology, and the dehumanizing impact of bureaucracy. The fundamental role of the Christian Church, then, in the post-Holocaust world is to announce with renewed zeal the truth that the Kingdom of God is not of this world, lest we confuse the human pursuit of political action with God's salvation and fall prey to new and perhaps more terrible idols in the future. We need to hear less of "creative" theology, which, as theology, seems to regularly lose those distinctions between the Creator and the created order that keeps the world and its systems in perspective. We must recognize that, at some point, political allegiances must give way and come under that higher Allegiance, which is the joy and opportunity of worshipping the eternal God "who alone has immortality and dwells in unapproachable light, whom no man has ever seen or can see. To him be honor and eternal dominion. Amen" (1 Tim. 6:11–16).

Endnotes

1. Ayn Rand, *Introduction to Objectivist Epistemology*, 2d ed., ed. Harry Binswanger and Leonard Peikoff (New York: Meridian Books, 1990), 1–3.

2. Adolf Hitler, *Mein Kampf*, trans. James Murphy (London: Hurst and Blackett, Ltd., 1939), 108–9.

3. Roger Kimball, *Tenured Radicals: How Politics Has Corrupted Our Higher Education* (New York: Harper Perennial Books, 1991), 102.

4. George Steiner, *Real Presences* (Chicago: University of Chicago Press, 1989), 119.

5. Ibid., 120.

6. Diane Ravitch, "Multiculturalism: E Pluribus Plures," *The Key Reporter*, vol. 56 (Autumn, 1990): 2.

7. John J. Miller, "Afrocentrism in the Suburbs," *National Review*, vol. 45, 18 (20 September 1993): 60.

8. Arthur M. Schlesinger, Jr., *The Disuniting of America: Reflections on a Multicultural Society* (New York: W.W. Norton and Company, 1992), 102.

9. Gene Edward Veith, Jr., *Modern Fascism: Liquidating the Judeo-Christian Worldview* (St. Louis: Concordia Publishing House, 1993), 23.

10. Sidney Hook, "Civilization and Its Malcontents," *National Review*, vol. 41, no. 19 (13 October 1989): 33.

11. Michael Howard, "Facing The Monsters," *The New York Times Book Review* (6 March 1994): 12.

12. For an extensive discussion of the "medicalization of anti-semitism," and the process of justifying the destruction of "lives not worth living," see Robert Proctor, *Racial Hygiene: Medicine under the Nazis* (Cambridge, Massachusetts: Harvard University Press, 1988), 177–222.

13. Robert Jay Lifton, *The Nazi Doctors: Medical Killing and the Psychology of Genocide* (New York: Basic Books, Inc., Publishers, 1986), 51–61.

14. See Dr. Wendell W. Watters, "Christianity and Mental Health," *The Humanist*, vol. 47, no. 6 (November/December, 1987): 5–11.

Dr. Watters sees Christian faith as destructive to mental health. His article is balanced by the perspectives of an accompanying article by Peter R. Breggin, "Mental Health Versus Religion," 12–13.

15. Edward R. Norman, "A Politicized Christ," *Christianity and Crisis*, vol. 39, no. 2 (19 February 1979): 18.

16. Arthur C. Cochrane, "Bonhoeffer and Barth vs. Norman," *Christianity and Crisis*, vol. 39, no. 6 (16 April 1979): 86.

17. Umberto Belli, *Breaking Faith: The Sandinista Revolution and Its Impact on Christian Faith in Nicaragua* (Westchester, Illinois: Crossway Books, 1985), 140–56.

18. Ibid., 51.

19. Ibid., 140.

20. Ibid., 159–60.

21. Photographs and discussions of these works were included in the December, 1989 *Prayer and News Letter* of Carribean Christian Ministries, Pompano Beach, Florida.

22. "A Controverted Conference," *The Christian Century*, vol. 111, no. 5 (16 February 1994): 161.

23. Louis L. Snyder, ed., *Hitler's Third Reich: A Documentary History* (Chicago: Nelson Hall Inc., 1981), 168.

24. Glenn Tinder, "Can We Be Good Without God?" *The Atlantic*, vol. 264, no. 6 (December, 1989): 68-85.

25. These elements were outlined in materials for public school teachers in Lincoln, Nebraska, pertaining to "New Age" education.

26. "The Culture of Apathy," *The New Republic*, vol. 198, no. 6 (8 February 1988): 7.

27. Jean-Francois Revel, *The Totalitarian Temptation* (New York: Doubleday and Company, Inc., 1977), 255.

28. Leszek Kolakowski, "The Idolatry Of Politics," *The New Republic*, vol. 194, no. 24 (16 June 1986): 31.

29. Ibid.

30. William Norman Grigg, "Hyping Hillary," *The New American*, vol. 9, no. 14 (12 July 1993): 5-6.

31. Leon Wieseltier, "Total Quality Meaning," *The New Republic*, vol. 209, no. 3/4 (19 July 1993): 20.

32. Ibid., 21–25.

33. Hitler, *Mein Kampf*, 168–69.

34. Zygmunt Bauman, *Modernity and the Holocaust* (Ithaca, New York: Cornell University Press, 1989), 91.

35. Page Smith, *Killing the Spirit* (New York: Viking Press, 1990), 168.

36. Ibid., 173.

37. Peter Russell, *The Global Brain* (Los Angeles: J.P. Tarcher, Inc., 1983), 97.

38. Ibid., 98–100.

39. Ibid., 130.

40. See "Karma for Cash: A 'New Age' for Workers?" *Christianity Today* (17 June 1988); Jeremy Mains, "Trying To Bend Managers' Minds," *Fortune* (23 November 1987); Annetta Miller and Pamela Abramson, "Corporate Mind Control," *Newsweek* (4 May 1987).

41. Walter Berns, "The New Pacifism and World Government," *National Review*, vol. XXXV, no. 10 (27 May 1983): 613–20.

42. Ibid.

43. William F. Jasper, *Global Tyranny . . . Step by Step: The United Nations and the Emerging New World Order* (Appleton, Wisconsin: Western Islands, 1992), 212. The quote was shared by Donald Keys, president of Planetary Citizens, at a symposium on Global Society held in Asheville, N.C. on 11 November 1984.

44. Robert Muller, *New Genesis: Shaping a Global Spirituality* (Garden City, New York: Doubleday and Company, Inc.), 142.

45. James Billington, *Fire in the Minds of Men: Origins of the Revolutionary Faith* (New York: Basic Books, 1980), 3.

46. Jeane Kirkpatrick, *Dictatorships and Double Standards: Rationalism and Reason in Politics* (New York: American Enterprise Institute, 1982), 96–119.

47. Richard M. Bucke, *Cosmic Consciousness* (New York: The Citadel Press, 1961), 5.

48. John Randolph Price, *The Superbeings* (New York: Fawcett Crest Books, 1981), 36.

49. Bauman, *Modernity and the Holocaust*, 92.

50. Ralph C. Hancock, "Robspierre and the Rights Of Man," *Policy Review* 49 (Summer, 1989): 40

51. Hermann Rauschning, *The Voice of Destruction* (New York: G.P. Putnam's Sons, 1940), 246.

52. William E. Hordern, *A Layman's Guide to Protestant Theology*, rev. ed. (New York: Macmillan Publishing Company, 1968), 135.

53. Rabbi Joshua O. Haberman, "The Bible Belt Is America's Safety Belt," *Policy Review* 42 (Fall, 1987): 40–44.

54. Ibid., 40.

55. Ibid., 41.

56. Charles P. Alexander, "A Parent's View of Pop Sex and Violence," *Time* (7 April 1990): 100.

57. Jeffrey Burton Russell, *The Prince of Darkness* (Ithaca, New York: Cornell University Press, 1988), 206–7.

Select Bibliography

Angebert, Jean-Michel. *The Occult and the Third Reich: The Mystical Origins of Nazism and the Search for the Holy Grail*. New York: Macmillan Publishing Co., 1974.

Arendt, Hannah. *Antisemitism*. New York: Harcourt, Brace and World, Inc., 1968.

Bauman, Zygmunt. *Modernity and the Holocaust*. Ithaca, New York: Cornell University Press, 1989.

Belli, Humberto. *Breaking Faith: The Sandinista Revolution and Its Impact on Christian Faith in Nicaragua*. Westchester, Illinois: Crossway Books, 1985.

Ben-Sasson, H.H. *A History of the Jewish People*. Cambridge, Massachusetts: Harvard University Press, 1976.

Blavatsky, Helena. *The Secret Doctrine*. vol. 3. 1897. Reprint. Wheaton, Illinois: Theosophical Publishing House, 1971.

Brown, Raymond. *The Anchor Bible: Commentary on the Gospel of John*. Vol. 1. New York: Doubleday, 1966.

Chamberlain, Houston Stewart. *The Foundations of the Nineteenth Century*. Translated by John Lees. New York: John Lane Company, 1910.

Cohen, Arthur A. *The Myth of the Judeo-Christian Tradition*. New York: Harper and Row, 1970.

Conway, J.S. *The Nazi Persecution of the Churches: 1933–1945.* New York: Basic Books, 1968.

Goodrick-Clarke, Nicholas. *The Occult Roots of Nazism: The Ariosophists of Austria and Germany, 1890–1935.* Wellingborough, Northamptonshire: The Aquarian Press, 1985.

Gutteridge, Richard. *Open Thy Mouth for the Dumb.* Oxford: Basil Blackwell, 1976.

Heiden, Konrad. *Der Fuehrer.* New York: Lexington Press, 1944.

Hertzberg, Arthur. *The French Enlightenment and the Jews.* New York: Columbia University Press, 1968.

Hitler, Adolf. *Mein Kampf.* Translated and annotated by James Murphy. London: Hurst and Blackett, Ltd., 1939.

Hordern, William. *A Layman's Guide to Protestant Theology.* New York: Macmillan Company, 1968.

Hubben, William. *Dostoevsky, Kiekegaard, Nietzsche, and Kafka: Four Prophets of Our Destiny.* New York: Collier Books, 1962.

Inge, Jens, ed. *At the Heart of the White Rose.* Translated by J. Maxwell Brownjohn. New York: Harper and Row, 1987.

Jacobsen, Hans-Adolf. *July 20, 1944: The German Opposition to Hitler as Viewed by Foreign Historians.* Wiesbaden: Press and Information Office of the Federal Government of Germany, Public Document, 1969.

Johnson, Paul. *A History of Christianity.* New York: Atheneum, 1976.

Kahler, Erich. *Man the Measure.* Cleveland: World Publishing Company, 1943.

Kaufmann, Walter. *The Portable Nietzsche.* New York: The Viking Press, 1954.

Kirkpatrick, Jeane J. *Dictatorships and Double Standards: Rationalism and Reason in Politics.* New York: American Enterprise Institute, 1982.

Lifton, Robert Jay. *The Nazi Doctors: Medical Killing and the Psychology of Genocide.* New York: Basic Books, Inc., 1986.

Littell, Franklin Hamlin. *The German Phoenix.* Garden City, New York: Doubleday and Company, 1960.

Mosse, George L. *The Crisis of German Ideology.* New York: Grosset and Dunlap, 1964.

Muller, Robert. *New Genesis: Shaping a Global Spirituality.* Garden City, New York: Doubleday and Company, Inc., 1984.

Nisbet, Robert. *History of the Idea of Progress.* New York: Basic Books, 1977.

Pauwels, Louis and Jacques Bergier. *The Morning of the Magicians.* Translated by Rollo Myers. Chelsea, Michigan: Scarborough House Publishers, 1991.

Peikoff, Leonard. *The Ominous Parallels.* New York: New American Library, 1982.

Prager, Dennis and Joseph Telushkin. *Why the Jews?* New York: Simon and Schuster, 1983.

Proctor, Robert. *Racial Hygiene: Medicine Under the Nazis.* Cambridge, Massachusetts: Harvard University Press, 1988.

Rand, Ayn. *Introduction to Objectivist Epistemology,* 2d ed. Edited by Harry Brinswanger and Leonard Peikoff. New York: The Penguin Group, 1990.

Rauschning, Hermann. *The Voice of Destruction.* New York: G.P. Putnam's Sons, 1940.

Remak, Joachim. *The Nazi Years: A Documentary History.* New York: Simon and Schuster, 1969.

Robertson, E.H. *Dietrich Bonhoeffer.* Richmond, Virginia: John Knox Press, 1966.

Rubenstein, Richard. *After Auschwitz.* Indianapolis: Bobbs-Merrill, 1966.

Ruhm von Oppen, Beate. *Religion and Resistance to Nazism.* Princeton, New Jersey: Princeton University, 1971.

Sandmel, Samuel. *A Jewish Understanding of the New Testament.* New York: KTAV Publishing House, 1974.

Sandmel, Samuel. *We Jews and Jesus*. New York: Oxford University Press, 1965.

Shirer, William L. *The Rise and Fall of the Third Reich*. New York: Simon and Schuster, 1960.

Smith, Page. *Killing the Spirit*. New York: Viking Press, 1990.

Snyder, Louis L. *Hitler's Third Reich: A Documentary History*. Chicago: Nelson Hall, Inc., 1981.

Speer, Albert. *Inside the Third Reich*. Translated by Richard and Clara Winston. New York: Macmillan Company, 1970.

Steiner, George. *Real Presences*. Chicago: University of Chicago Press, 1989.

Stern, Fritz. *The Politics of Cultural Despair: A Study in the Rise of the German Ideology*. Berkeley and Los Angeles: University of California Press, 1961.

Suster, Gerald. *Hitler: The Occult Messiah*. New York: St. Martin's Press, 1981.

The Third Reich. (A study published under the auspices of the International Council for Philosophy and Humanistic Studies and with the assistance of UNESCO). New York: Frederick A. Praeger, 1955.

Veith, Jr., Gene Edward. *Modern Fascism: Liquidating the Judeo-Christian Worldview*. St. Louis: Concordia Publishing House, 1993.

Viereck, Peter. *Meta-Politics: The Roots of the Nazi Mind*. New York: Capricorn Books, 1965.

Waite, Robert G.L. *The Psychopathic God: Adolf Hitler*. New York: Basic Books, 1977.

More Good Books from Huntington House

The Liberal Contradiction
by Dale A. Berryhill

Why are liberals who took part in student demonstrations in the 1960s now trying to stop Operation Rescue from using the very same tactics? Liberalism claims to advocate some definite moral positions: racism and sexism are wrong; tolerance is right; harming the environment is wrong; protecting it is right. But, contemporary liberalism is undermining its own moral foundation. It contends that its positions are morally right and the opposites are wrong, while at the same time, it denies that a moral law (right and wrong) exists. This is the **Liberal Contradiction** and it leads to many ludicrous (and laughable) inconsistencies.

ISBN 1-56384-055-3 $9.99

Conservative, American & Jewish—
I Wouldn't Have It Any Other Way
by Jacob Neusner

Neusner has fought on the front lines of the culture war and here writes reports about sectors of the battles. He has taken a consistent, conservative position in the academy, federal agencies in the humanities and the arts, and in the world of religion in general and Judaism in particular. Engaging, persuasive, controversial in the best sense, these essays set out to change minds and end up touching the hearts and souls of their readers.

ISBN 1-56384-048-0 $9.99

Political Correctness:
The Cloning of the American Mind
by David Thibodaux, Ph.D.

The author, a professor of literature at the University of Southwestern Louisiana, confronts head on the movement that is now being called Political Correctness. Political correctness, says Thibodaux, "is an umbrella under which advocates of civil rights, gay and lesbian rights, feminism, and environmental causes have gathered." To incur the wrath of these groups, one only has to disagree with them on political, moral, or social issues. To express traditionally Western concepts in universities today can result in not only ostracism, but even suspension. (According to a recent "McNeil-Lehrer News Hour" report, one student was suspended for discussing the reality of the moral law with an avowed homosexual. He was reinstated only after he apologized.)

ISBN 1-56384-026-X Trade Paper $9.99

Beyond Political Correctness:
Are There Limits to This Lunacy?
by David Thibodaux, Ph.D.

Author of the best-selling *Political Correctness: The Cloning of the American Mind,* Dr. David Thibodaux now presents his long awaited sequel—*Beyond Political Correctness: Are There Limits to This Lunacy?* The politically correct movement has now moved beyond college campuses. The movement has succeeded in turning the educational system of this country into a system of indoctrination. Its effect on education was predictable: steadily declining scores on every conceivable test which measures student performance; and, increasing numbers of college freshmen who know a great deal about condoms, homosexuality, and abortion, but whose basic skills in language, math, and science are alarmingly deficient.

ISBN 1-56384-066-9 $9.99

A Jewish Conservative
Looks at Pagan America
by Don Feder

With eloquence and insight that rival contemporary commentators and essayists of antiquity, Don Feder's pen finds his targets in the enemies of God, family, and American tradition and morality. Deftly . . . delightfully . . . the master allegorist and Titian with a typewriter brings clarity to the most complex sociological issues and invokes giggles and wry smiles from both followers and foes. Feder is Jewish to the core, and he finds in his Judaism no inconsistency with an American Judeo-Christian ethic. Questions of morality plague school administrators, district court judges, senators, congressmen, parents, and employers; they are wrestling for answers in a "changing world." Feder challenges this generation and directs inquirers to the original books of wisdom: the Torah and the Bible.

ISBN 1-56384-036-7 Trade Paper $9.99
ISBN 1-56384-037-5 Hardcover $19.99

Out of Control—
Who's Watching Our Child
Protection Agencies?
by Brenda Scott

This book of horror stories is true. The deplorable and unauthorized might of Child Protection Services is capable of reaching into and destroying any home in America. No matter how innocent and happy your family may be, you are one accusation away from disaster. Social workers are allowed to violate constitutional rights and often become judge, jury, and executioner. Innocent parents may appear on computer registers and be branded "child abuser" for life. Every year, it is estimated that over 1 million people are falsely accused of child abuse in this country. You could be next, says author and speaker Brenda Scott.

ISBN 1-56384-069-3 $9.99

ORDER THESE HUNTINGTON HOUSE BOOKS !

____	America: Awaiting the Verdict—Mike Fuselier	4.99 ____
____	America Betrayed—Marlin Maddoux	6.99 ____
____	Beyond Political Correctness—David Thibodaux	9.99 ____
____	A Call to Manhood—David E. Long	9.99 ____
____	Conservative, American & Jewish—Jacob Neusner	9.99 ____
____	The Dark Side of Freemasonry—Ed Decker	9.99 ____
____	Deadly Deception: Freemasonry—Tom McKenney	8.99 ____
____	Don't Touch That Dial—Barbara Hattemer & Robert Showers	9.99/19.99 ____
____	En Route to Global Occupation—Gary Kah	9.99 ____
____	*Exposing the AIDS Scandal—Dr. Paul Cameron	7.99/2.99 ____
____	The Extermination of Christianity—Paul Schenck	9.99 ____
____	Freud's War with God—Jack Wright, Jr.	7.99 ____
____	Goddess Earth—Samantha Smith	9.99 ____
____	Gays & Guns—John Eidsmoe	7.99/14.99 ____
____	Heresy Hunters—Jim Spencer	8.99 ____
____	Hidden Dangers of the Rainbow—Constance Cumbey	9.99 ____
____	Hitler and the New Age—Bob Rosio	9.99 ____
____	Homeless in America—Jeremy Reynalds	9.99 ____
____	How to Homeschool (Yes, You!)—Julia Toto	4.99 ____
____	*Inside the New Age Nightmare—Randall Baer	9.99/2.99 ____
____	A Jewish Conservative Looks at Pagan America—Don Feder	9.99/19.99 ____
____	Kinsey, Sex and Fraud—Dr. Judith A. Reisman &	11.99 ____
	Edward Eichel (Hard cover)	
____	The Liberal Contradiction—Dale A. Berryhill	7.99 ____
____	Legalized Gambling—John Eidsmoe	9.99 ____
____	Loyal Opposition—John Eidsmoe	8.99 ____
____	The Media Hates Conservatives—Dale A. Berryhill	9.99 ____
____	Out of Control—Brenda Scott	9.99 ____
____	Please Tell Me—Tom McKenney	9.99 ____
____	Political Correctness—David Thibodaux	9.99 ____
____	Prescription Death—Dr. Reed Bell & Frank York	9.99 ____
____	*The Question of Freemasonry—Ed Decker	2.99 ____
____	Real Men—Dr. Harold Voth	9.99 ____
____	"Soft Porn" Plays Hardball—Dr. Judith A. Reisman	8.99/16.99 ____
____	Subtle Serpent—Darylann Whitemarsh & Bill Reisman	9.99 ____
____	Teens and Devil Worship—Charles Evans	8.99 ____
____	*To Moroni With Love—Ed Decker	2.99 ____
____	Trojan Horse—Brenda Scott & Samantha Smith	9.99 ____
____	When the Wicked Seize a City—Chuck & Donna McIlhenny	9.99 ____
	with Frank York	

*Available in Salt Series

Shipping & Handling ____
TOTAL ____

AVAILABLE AT BOOKSTORES EVERYWHERE or order direct from:
Huntington House Publishers • P.O. Box 53788 • Lafayette, LA 70505
Send check/money order. For faster service use VISA/MASTERCARD
Call toll-free 1-800-749-4009.
Add: Freight and handling, $3.50 for the first book ordered, and $.50 for
each additional book up to 5 books.

Enclosed is $_____including postage.
VISA/MASTERCARD #_____ Exp. Date _____
Name_____ Phone: (   ) _____
Address_____
City, State, Zip_____